# Editorial

It is both the joy and the challenge of editing a literary magazine to maintain an identity while constantly evolving. Perhaps that is also the joy and challenge of being a writer: while a strong, distinctive voice can define a body of work, few writers – and readers – would enjoy the same story, told repeatedly the same way. We love discovering new voices for *Gutter*, but are equally excited when familiar voices say something unexpected or find new ways to speak.

In recent issues *Gutter* has concentrated on fiction and poetry rather than creative non-fiction. Issue 11 rectifies that with two striking pieces. In 'Oona', Eleanor Thom gives a moving and honest account of the ill health of her baby daughter, and Lynnda Wardle varies the theme in an extract from 'Acacia Gardens', her touching memoir of her parents' decisions around adopting a child. As we have found over the past ten issues, often a subconscious theme emerges to link works that we have selected. This time, startlingly different perspectives of parenthood run through narratives by Kirsty Gunn, Nick Brooks, and Vicki Jarrett.

This issue also includes fresh perspectives on our social and technological trajectory from Ever Dundas, Mike Russell and Lynsey May; while two writers better known for their poetry and flash fiction respectively – Colin Herd and Dan Spencer – both turn to longer prose forms with wonderfully visual results.

*Gutter* is resolute in its commitment to remain Scottish *and* international, so we are particularly pleased to bring you new work from one of Tunisia's leading young writers, Rached Khalifa, whose take on censorship after the Arab Spring ('Ants') is at once both chilling and hopeful. It also reminds us how far our own society has traveled in the past 40 years in respecting freedom of expression. Last month saw the death of irrepressible poet and publisher Felix Dennis, of *Oz* magazine and *Viz* comic amongst others, whose 1970s trial for 'Conspiracy to deprave and corrupt the Morals of the Young of the Realm' changed Britain's absurd censorship laws and allowed the subsequent explosion of challenging literary, musical and cinematic themes.

Dennis also has the distinction of being the first person to use the word 'cunt' live on British television (in reference to Jerry Rubin), but without him there might have been no *Trainspotting*, no *How Late it Was, How Late*, no *Never Mind the Bollocks*, no *My Beautiful Launderette*, no *Satanic Verses*. In a time where the state and other actors are attempting to roll back these hard-won liberties in the name of security, it is worth honouring Dennis's legacy to us all.

We are glad to welcome two outstanding poets to these pages for the first time. Much of Tom Pow's previous work has made an art of themes of dislocation, isolation and exile, and he continues to do so in his series of prose poems 'Notes from a Dying Village'. A different perspective on small town ennui is given by Roddy Lumsden's 'Bad Players' and 'Towns you Only Pass Through'.

Other poets making their *Gutter* debut include Robert James Berry, Jane Bonnyman, and Ciara McLaverty; and there is new work from *Gutter* regulars Jim Ferguson, Graham Fulton, Andy Jackson, Rob A Mackenzie, and Jim Carruth – to whom we offer our warmest congratulations on his recent appointment as Glasgow's new Poet Laureate. There is also an excellent three-way, three-poem English-Scots-Gaelic translation collaboration from AC Clarke, Sheila Templeton and Maggie Rabatski.

Outwith its socio-economic needs, Scotland's difference from the rest of the United Kingdom is nowhere more strongly apparent that in its literature, language and poetry – the renaissance of which kick-started the Scottish nationalist (note the small 'n') movement in the 1940s.

Many of us in the 'cultural sector' (this editorial team included) have long adhered to Alasdair Gray's dictum, 'Work as though you live in the early days of a better nation' – but we cultural *arbeiters* can be guilty of a cosy complacency from being largely surrounded by those who share our view that Scotland's economic and cultural future is better secured by independence from the United Kingdom.

We are not yet the majority – believe the polls, they are consistent – so it is imperative that we get out there and persuade others, politely and reasonably, that our vision of Scotland's future is the most appropriate one for Scotland's economic, geographical and cultural circumstances. In doing so, we should emphasise that this issue transcends party politics. To paraphrase George Orwell: 'Political Language... of all parties... is designed to make lies sound truthful... and to give an appearance of solidity to pure wind.'

As Wendy Miller's poem on p103 tells us, we must "opt to see through the mist". We must show our fellow voters the true wind direction, and let them grasp the truth from the way each side tells lies.

# Ants

*Rached Khalifa*

It all started when he found it difficult to fall asleep. His mind would filter pages and pages of black print he had read during the day in search of details he had overlooked. What if that word meant this instead of that? What if that phrase were ironic? He should have branded that book UNDESIRABLE. He would do it tomorrow, but he had to read the text again. In the meantime books were piling up on his desk. He found it more and more daunting to catch up with the flow. Details were too many. He would read and reread with little progress. Every detail was a booby trap. He was treading on minefields. As soon as he turned over a word an explosion of connections, like shrapnel, would blast his mind and shatter the tranquility of his conscience. Meanings would lead into meanings, connections into connections. He couldn't walk further. Yet he had to walk on. The future of the nation relied on the diligence of people like him. The black print filled his brain like ants infesting a tree bark. His head turned into an anthill.

When he went home after work he would lie on the bed, exhausted and dreading the night. He had lost appetite for food and sex and sleep. He had lost desire altogether. His mind was a whirlwind of words. They crammed his brain. He couldn't fall asleep. He would recite the same Koranic verses to chase the ants out of his head. *When they came to a valley of ants, one of the ants said: 'O ye ants, get into your habitations, lest Solomon and his hosts crush you under foot without knowing it.'*

The holy words wouldn't silence the din in his head. His wife would dab his forehead with Vicks and rosewater. They wouldn't work. His eyes would remain wide open until the ceiling and walls blurred and turned into a giant paper upon which his internal text imprinted itself. The black lines would stream on the white ceiling like surtitles, erratic and schizophrenic. When he closed his eyes it became worse. He would see the mural print impress itself onto his mental one and both texts would merge in a smudge of black ink with shooting tiny legs. The unintelligibility of the smudge would sear his brain like a red-hot rod. He would feel it burn into the core of his brain. He would bark out at his wife to turn off the lights. Obsequiously she would. The darkness would bring only a momentary relief. Soon the black words would grow wiry legs, pinchers and antennae and start to work into his brain. They would cut into its soggy matter with their metallic mandibles and carve out bits and pieces they carried nowhere. Their legs dipped in his swampy brain and their antennae twitched in excitement over its sluicing juices. They scuttled in and out of its porous matter. They rustled and pricked his head. He felt his brain frittering, eaten away morsel by morsel. He couldn't bear the pain anymore. His wife felt helpless. His children immured themselves in their rooms, listless and ashen.

Late at night, when silence fell upon the house, the ant colony would scurry out of his head and invade his thorax, abdomen, and limbs. Their hustle and bustle sent a shiver all over his body before his skin started to deaden. He pinched himself but his skin felt numb and uncanny, not part of him. The numbness sent him half-asleep. A crushing weight smothered his chest. He couldn't tell what it was. He gasped for breath and tried to push it away with what energy remained in him. Nothing happened. The weight lingered. He grew alarmingly out of breath. Instinctively, he jolted and began to wiggle himself out from underneath the weight. He inched his way sideways, like a crab, his body leaden and disjointed, but his fingers clawed into the mattress. He fell off the bed and thudded onto the bare floor. His back landed first. His body wobbled for a moment then stabilised at the epicenter of his back, now curved like the carcass of some giant crustacean. His limbs flailed uncontrollably as though ruptured from his nerve center. Then they curled and rigidified like twigs. He tried to stand up but only wobbled on his back. He tried to flip onto his right side and push himself up with both hands, but he couldn't move. His body was dead like a capsized turtle. 'The lights! The lights, for God's sake!' His words rang bizarrely in his ears, more animal squeak than human voice. Was he morphing into another creature? Was he turning into a giant beetle? Was it Kafka's revenge, after all?

A few days before, he had sent the man into the furnace. He had read *Metamorphosis* a couple of times, but his verdict was irrevocable—

'Send the fucking Jew to the crematorium! He slights God's wisdom.'

With his red stamp he smeared the virginal flyleaf – UNDESIRABLE.

His wife turned on the lights. He was frozen in his crustacean position, his head tilted to the ceiling, his back arched upwards, his limbs and fingers autumnal twigs, arthritic and xyloid. She was horrified. She tucked her arms under his neck and knees and hoisted him onto the bed. He was a dead log. She dabbed his forehead with rosewater and kept massaging his limbs until they began to loosen at dawn.

He has made up his mind this time. Tomorrow he will do it, there in front of the Town Hall, at the rush hour. That's the best time. Nothing can make him change his mind. He's mulled over the idea for a while. It's ripe. It won't be as improvised as the one that took place twenty years ago. This time it is planned.

He had graduated years before. He studied History. But like thousands of fellow graduates he found no job after graduation. His dream of a decent life was shattered when he had to go home and depend on his parents. His frustration poisoned his life. He had a degree in his bag but no money in his pocket. The villagers mocked him. They derided his degree. History, huh, who cares about history today? How can History make you win your bread? Why didn't you study banking or accountancy or engineering? He was tired of their battering questions and sardonic eyes. He lost faith in what he did. After all, what could History do for him?

He did petty jobs. Then he worked as a shepherd when his father fell ill. He tended sheep and goats on sun-scorched steppes. The work gave him ample time to ponder over his depleted life, as depleted as the steppes around him. He had dreamt of an office and a salary and city life. All these years spent on understanding the essence of history dwindled to clicking and shushing sheep.

His misery had lasted for years, until that great act of improvised self-sacrifice that turned the world upside down. The dictator fled the country and the Arab Spring kicked in. Like sandcastles dictatorial regimes across the Arab world crumbled under the tumult of people's anger and revolt. He couldn't find the words to describe his feeling that day. No fear after today, the people chanted. They danced and sang and hugged and kissed in the streets. Neighbours shared food and exchanged good mornings. People queued and stopped at traffic lights. Children planted roses in gun barrels. Euphoria suffused the air. The day the dictator had fled inaugurated a new age of liberty, dignity and civility.

That day he lost a friend. He was shot dead a few inches away from him. They had taken to the streets like thousands of demonstrators. The gates of history were forced open. This is the History he had studied in books. This is History transmuting itself into flesh and blood. The image of his friend prostrate on the ground, shirt smeared with blood and mud, and bits and pieces of flesh and bone and brain scattered on the asphalt remained with him all his life. That day he vowed to avenge his friend.

He joined the local Revolution Protection League. He espoused its noble mission. Its members organized mass events, prayers, and parades. They stayed all night watching over neighbourhoods. Their mission was history-making, he thought. They fought the counter-revolutionary forces. The Revolution was in its infancy and they had to protect the infant. They had to be vigilant. They prayed and trained in secret camps. They mounted guard in every corner, for the enemies lurked in every corner.

He grew a beard. He tended it every morning. When he didn't he didn't feel good.

Elections came. His Party won. He celebrated the triumph with his friends in the League. Finally the country made peace with culture, history, and faith. No Western rubbish anymore.

He watched, prayed, trained and trimmed his beard until one day the Party broke the news to him. He was offered a job in the capital. *Viva la revolución!* His dream of a decent life finally came true. His education had served him at last. He would put his skills at the service of the nascent nation.

He packed and headed for the big city.

He started as Head of the Book Boosting Board (BBB). Its mission was to promote revolutionary works and counter dangerous literature. Some Party officials suggested the name Book Censorship Board, but the majority shrugged it off on grounds that it was demeaning to the spirit of the Revolution. Their mission was to purify, not to censor.

The job was not challenging. It was rather boring. There was no intellectual stimulus. Trucks filled with old regime literature were unloaded on the cement square inside the building.

The smell of burned paper nauseated him at the beginning, but later, strangely, it became sweetness in the nostrils.

Later there came in genuine literature. He had to confine himself to his tiny office and read through stacks of books to look for insidious language. The Revolution had to immunise itself against its enemies. Explicit meanings were not a challenge, but the hidden ones were daunting, although more exciting to decipher. The enemies lurked not in the literal but in the metaphorical. They concealed themselves in thickets of figures, in allegories and metaphors. His job gained something of the excitement of game hunting. Tease meanings out of the thicket and shoot them down like squealing rabbits or boars. Send the bastards to hell.

The task became titanic in keeping with the Revolution's growing ambitions. All literature had to be sifted through, past and present and future, old and new, canonical and non-canonical, ante-Islamic and post-Islamic, Arab and non-Arab, original and translated, children books and strip cartoons, old manuscripts, treatises, poetry collections, fiction, drama, illustrated books, theses, journals. There should be no remorse over expunging this literature. It had soiled the soul of the nation for centuries. If we are what we are it is because of this sick literature. Revolutions start with *tabula rasa*. The slate must be clean.

Mountains of books were unloaded every day to go up in smoke. So much commitment, so much excitement!

He would spend hours reading thousands of black words until they danced before his eyes like crazy ants. The lines would intertwine and part, collide and collude. He would nonetheless read on. He had a mission, and a strong sense of duty too. His eyes deteriorated. The neon light seared them. They itched, burned, welled, and blurred. He had to read and reread words, sentences, and paragraphs, to understand what they meant to make sure they did not betray the spirit of the Revolution. Yes he had to be fair with books. The Revolution was after all moral.

He wasted more time on poetry. Why should poets complicate things? The ideals of the Revolution are simple, though. Why shouldn't they simply sing its goals? Why shouldn't they celebrate our nascent Islamic *ummah*? Why shouldn't they hail our leaders and heroes?

He branded collections UNDESIRABLE. Even the work of the national poet went into the crematorium. *If one day the people will life, Fate must give in to the strife!* How could people accept such sacrilegious rubbish?

He married and fathered lots of children for the *ummah*.

That morning he felt sick. His head ached from sleep deprivation. When he walked into his office he had no energy for reading. He would have perhaps tolerated a light thing. But on his desk was Kant towering up and regarding him. Shit, he's a bore. He's a degenerate like all modern Western philosophers. Their obsession with reason is deleterious to the nation. He flipped open his ink box, dislodged his rectangular stamp from its groove and pressed it hard onto the ink-soaked pad. Red ink oozed out from underneath the wooden edges. He had no mind for Kant that morning. He would send him to ash and smoke. He grabbed the book on the top, turned the cover and lowered his hand to stamp the flyleaf. But it hung in the air, hesitant and shaky. What made him stop? Was it the rashness of his decision? Was it his conscience?

He had to read a passage or two at least to justify his decision to himself. He slid the stamp back into the groove, sank in his fake leather armchair and leafed through the book. His eyes fell on *What is Enlightenment?* A few pages to read. They would be enough to justify his decision. No qualms after that.

As he furrows through the crowd, past him brush bodies hidden in *niqabs*. A thought crosses his mind. What if he stripped naked in this world of dissimulation? Nakedness is after all an act of absolute freedom in this world of concealment. The idea strikes him as most subversive. The mystery of the world lies in the visible. He has read this somewhere. His mind was too busy to remember where. Pathological concealment feeds pathological fantasy. The hidden whets the libidinal. Don't they know this? It has nothing to do with religious piety. It is the work of optics and psychics. Even God has envisaged a fig leaf, not a bin bag. Would God care about a square inch of flesh exposed or hidden? The whole thing sounds ridiculous to him now. He thinks of unbuttoning his jacket and cry out *I choose to be naked in a society where mullahs dictate their dress codes.* But he changes his mind. He will be taken for a madman. And his plan will be thwarted.

*Sapere Aude* tormented his mind. He had to read the essay more than once. Hardly anything seeped into his mind. The stream of words cascaded over his brain, leaving no trace of meaning. He caught his eyes roaming across a sentence or a paragraph without understanding a thing. He had to read the text again with redoubled concentration. He adjusted himself in his armchair.

The text was now literally painful. He had to concentrate on every word and sentence. He felt the words dent his brain. He felt it physically. *Sapere Aude* hit his head like a hammer. His head throbbed. A faint thought, however, glowed in the core of his brain. It troubled his conscience. What if he has been all these years one of those guardians? A guardian to guard the Revolution, a guardian to guard God? What if he has been all these years himself a victim of self-incurred tutelage?

He shrugged off the thought. Preposterous. Unhesitatingly he stamped Kant into the furnace. A pure nation needed the passions of the heart. As more books were fed into the furnace, more piled up on his desk. But he was not in the mood for reading after Kant. The bastard had drained his brain. At six he left his office.

He drove home with mixed feelings. Contented and yet dissatisfied with his day's work. He hadn't read all Kant, and yet he had sent him to the furnace. He had somehow betrayed his professionalism. He had always been conscientious. As he lashed his conscience, *Sapere Aude* looped in his head like a defective CD. He surprised himself crooning the phrase through traffic jams, *SA-PE-RE AU-DE.* Each time he put the stress on a different syllable. He knew no Latin. To fend off the phrase he recited Koranic verses.

But the words stayed there, thumbed into his head like seeds into muck.

That night he didn't see or feel the ants. The smudge gave way to questions. His mind compulsively drilled *SA-PE-RE AU-DE*. The phrase throbbed in his brain like a fresh cut. Dare to know! But he knew; he knew too well even. His knowledge was imperturbable. His edifice could not be knocked down. Yet the questions kept ramming his head. What if what he knew was not the knowledge he had to know? No way, he was right, his mission was right, his faith was right. His knowledge was unshakable. But if his knowledge was unshakable, why should he fear shakable knowledge? What is shakable is shakable, corrupt corrupt. This is common sense. If he knows Ultimate Truth, why should he then fear bogus truth?

No, no, what he was doing he was doing it for the nation, for the Revolution, he countered. His release from the tangle made him smile. Yes, the people needed a guardian to show them the right path. Allah willed it, Allah wanted it. But does Allah need him as His guardian? The question slashed through his head. Does God need someone to defend Him? Is he not infantilizing God by deciding what is good for Him and what is not? Is he not playing God in his dull office? Does God really care about a metaphor in a line or a passage? Can God, this Absolute Power, be upset by a twist of a sentence?

The questions jabbed his mind. How could he dare raise such questions? Damn Kant!

The questions hammered his head for weeks. In the meantime he felt something like a growth sprout inside his head. He felt it botanically, like a dried tuber breaking through caked soil. As it grew, it pierced through layers of sediment and mud. It tore through cerebral neurons and opinions. Its leaves, albeit frail and velvety, ripped through hard mud. Coiled and introverted at the beginning, but as soon as they freed themselves from muck and mulch, they spread wide open, yearning for light and enlightenment. The feeling was not without pain – physical and moral. It frayed his conscience and overturned his caked convictions. It felt like rebirth. Since that day his world had turned upside down. He hit the point of no-return. His convictions disintegrated like a heap of sand hit by a sweeping wave. An inner voice grew and swelled and filled his head – Dare to know!

Tomorrow is finally here. December 17. Symbolism matters after all. This he has learned from poetry.

He courses his way through the crowd. He walks against the flow towards the Town Hall. It is the rush hour. That is his plan.

It is a glorious morning. The sky is cloudless. The sun has the thickness of an egg yolk. It hangs high upon a pristine blue backdrop. Thank God they can't tamper with it. He carries a plastic tank of paraffin. The liquid iridesces in the sunlight. A two-litre tank. It's enough. One cubic centimeter per ten square centimeters of derma.

A swallow darts from behind the glassy building and dances up and down in perfect choreography. It is the migration season, he remembers. The sight of this elegant tiny bird fills his heart with joy. He has read somewhere of the metempsychosis of birds. His spirit becomes lighter. Never has his body been lighter and his heart warmer. Something has thawed in him since that day. He feels he could soar like that swallow should he jump and spread and flutter his arms in the air.

He reaches the old city. The wide street, a remnant of French colonialism, bifurcates into two serpentine lanes which widen and narrow to the main square. They look cavernous from a distance. Both lanes lead to the Town Hall, but he chooses the one on the left-hand side. As soon as he walks into the tunnel-like lane, a throng of human bodies, like ants, swarm towards him, thrown out from the bowels of the medina. He keels into the flow, avoiding as much as possible contact with the people. Deformed by starch and decadence, the human shapes now assault his eyes. Pungent smells clog his nostrils and mind, the heavy smells of medieval perfumes, body odors and halitosis. They fill the air and hang like little clouds of vapor. He used to relish the place. But now the smells and mess of the souks nauseate him. The place has become a parody of national character, a farce taken seriously by the audience.

Women wobble down the lane. They look like huge bin bags, inflating and deflating in the rushing draughts. They trudge down, cautious not to trip over their frills. Their *niqabs* offer them a tiny aperture into the world. They peep, rather than see. They walk behind husbands with shifty eyes. The men, rough-hewn clay statues just unearthed from dust, wearing scruffy beards and baggy cloaks, flit here and there, from shop to shop. The scene is of another age, he thinks. Is it for all this that blood was shed? Is it for all this that the dream was dreamt?

The winding lane suddenly opens into a vast triangular square. Here on this hilly agglomeration of buildings, different architectural styles, testimonies of the country's histories, live together in perfect cohabitation. Architecture holds no grudge. It is like history—impersonal. Nations are made and unmade. History is a formidable weaver; architecture is its tapestry.

At the center of the vast square towers an imposing monument. Four colossal marble slabs aim at the sky, like a rocket on a launching pad,. The regime wants it to symbolize religious and economic takeoff. Not far behind it stands a no less imposing edifice—the Town Hall.

As he walks out of the lane and into the square he feels revived by the fresh air and the end of corporeal impediment. The sense of freedom rekindles his determination. He walks forward. The beginning of change is imminent. With his act he will set the nation's imagination ablaze again. Twenty years ago that poor young man had captivated the imagination of the people. His act had set the nation afire. But the dream of an Arab Spring, rolling over the Arab desert from the Atlantic to the Gulf, turned into a chilling winter. It was stilled where it was born. All that revolutionary bubble had fizzled out with petrodollars and geopolitics. Freedom was gagged, women veiled, alcohol banned, poverty justified, and strikes outlawed.

He walks up the few marble steps. He stands on the platform facing the sprawling city beneath. The oblong monument towers behind him. The city shimmers in the sun, enwrapped in the mist of its ignorance and anachronism. The areas surrounding him come into focus as he zooms around. The platform gives him a panoramic view. Behind the city stands Mount Baal Qarneen, the 'two-horned god,' a reminder of the country's ancient religions and myths.

*Your God is dead! Your Baal is dead!* He shouts at the top of his voice. *I don't believe in what you believe! I don't worship what you worship! We create the God we are! Oh People, it's time to dismantle your God of stone and spite. Worship the God in you. God is not fear! God is Love! God is Freedom! God is Humanity! Oh People, worship the Great God in you!*

He sees people gather around him. He then sings the old anthem, *If one day the people will life, Fate must give in to the strife!* Some voices chorus after him, timid at the beginning then gain in self-confidence.

Paraffin had a peculiar smell this time, intoxicating and hydromantic. He fumbled in his pocket. As smell and blaze coalesced in a dazzling ball of dancing flames, orangey and gooey, the full meaning of the lines he had read somewhere finally flared up in his mind: 'Arise and bid me strike a match/And strike another till time catch.'

He felt peace, roundness and something like a chill ripple through his skin.

# Camel

*Liam Murray Bell*

Massey comes in and sits in front of the guest ale pump. It's an IPA from Alloa. He ignores it and reaches across to tap at the Guinness one instead. His mother's family were from County Kerry and Massey drinks stout like it's a transfusion to top up his Irish blood. I wait for the pint to settle, then finish it off and set it in front of him. He turns the glass until the harp faces him and then looks up to meet my eye.

'Graeme,' he says. 'D'you know what a camel would be worth?'

'The animal?' I ask, stalling for time.

He nods. I pick up a glass to polish, looking across at Rebecca to see if she's listening in. She isn't. She never is.

'One hump or two?' I ask.

'Does it make a difference?'

I shrug. 'It just might, aye.'

'Two then.'

'No idea, Massey.'

'One?'

'Not a clue.'

Massey's real name is Ferguson. Surname that is. If he had a first name then it was forgotten a long time ago – replaced by the adopted name of a tractor brand. He's in every night, after a day of tending to his pigs, for his prescription of three supped pints.

It used to be that he'd chat to my wife, Rebecca, about farming. But then she took up painting. She stands, now, at the end of the bar with an easel set up, frowning at the canvas in front of her. She used to ask the regulars these bright questions – all about the subsidies, the harvest times, the strains of lambing season. Now she just stands silently, painting things that aren't even there. She sees men waiting at the bar as squares and triangles rather than as customers that need to be served.

'I might be able to help you out, Massey.'

This comes from a young schemie, Cleland, who is seated over by the fireplace with a group of folk he'd eagerly call friends but who'd be loath to repay the compliment. He rises from the table, prompting a collective sigh of relief that acts as a bellows for the fire in the grate.

'I have a pal in Dubai,' he says. 'I could give him a call.'

'Thanks,' Massey eyes him over the pint.

'Although the long distance call would cost me...'

'Much d'you want for it?'

'Two pints. Guest ale.'

I wait for the nod from Massey, then start pouring out the ale. It's the first from the keg, so it runs as foam. It looks like it should be served with a wafer and raspberry sauce. Cleland watches as I set the first attempt aside and start over.

The yellow-orange glow from the streetlight gleams off his jacket and trousers as he steps outside to make his call. It's more shell-suit than business attire, although he'd probably tell you it was from Perugia rather than Perth. Underneath, he's not much more than a rickle of bones, held in place by a clip-on tie at the neck and a tight-trussed belt, at the waist, that is no more leather than the suit is silk.

'Watch out for that one, Mass,' I say.

He nods, counts out the change for the pint.

'Why are you asking about a camel anyway?'

Massey tugs at his hair. As if it were a toupee and he wanted to check the hold of the adhesive. In the time I've known him, the red of his hair has turned grey. Not the light grey of the tractor he's named after, but a darker, dirtier shade. With streaks of red, like rust, still showing through on top.

'I'm selling the old Land Rover,' he says. 'And I had a gentleman up to the farm to see me about it. Young lad. Asked if I would be open to a trade – camel for a car.'

'Arab?'

'Eh?'

'Was he an Arab lad?'

Massey shrugs. 'He wasn't from around here.'

I consider all this. Most of the locals, including those who came from further afield originally, are known to me. Everyone from Denny to Bonnybridge. I can think of no-one – with the possible exception of Cleland – who'd know how to lay their hands on a camel.

I could ask Rebecca, of course, if she's heard a camel-seller mentioned during the quiet day-shifts. She's deep in her work, though – the tip of her tongue darting in and out of her mouth as if it's actually dabbing the paint onto the canvas.

'Do you think he was for real?' I ask.

'Seemed to be.'

'Straight swap?'

Massey nods. 'Camel for a car.'

There's a safari park on the other side of Stirling. If a camel had been nicked from there, though, then it would have been in the papers.

'Where's the camel now?' I ask.

'Mushroom farm, he said. Up near Arbroath.'

'Does a camel even eat mushrooms?'

Cleland comes back in. His swagger is wider – it threatens to spin him right around.

He birls up to the bar, takes a drink of his pint and pauses for effect. This is the most attention he's had since that Orangeman from Larbert left half his teeth on the pavement outside after he'd got the daughter – orange from the sunbeds – pregnant.

'Seven grand,' Cleland grins, showing his capped teeth. 'As long as it's in good condition.'

'Seven?' Massey asks.

'Aye. Maybe a grand either way, depending.'

'How much are you asking for the Land Rover?' I ask.

'Three,' Massey says. 'It's not in the best state.'

'Three against seven then,' I say.

'It seems it, aye.'

Cleland sits himself down, pulling his pint along the bar after him. Massey will pay more than the cost of two pints for the information. Cleland will be his companion for the rest of the evening.

'Massey,' I say, before the younger man starts yammering. 'There won't even be a camel. It'll all be a scam or a piss-take.'

'I'm not sure, like...'

'I'd put money on it.'

'How much?' Massey asks.

I look at Cleland, but don't ask for his valuation. Then I glance across at Rebecca, standing behind her easel. She used to disapprove of my betting. Odds are she won't notice, though. Not a wee flutter.

'Fifty quid,' I say.

Massey reaches across to shake my hand. Then, with the same movement, places a finger on the Guinness tap. I nod, smile. Even if there is a camel, even on that off-chance, it'll only take me a week to make my money back off Massey. There's little risk involved.

I count the notes out: one twenty, three crisp tens. I don't bother hiding them from Rebecca. Massey takes them with one hand and, with the other, holds his phone out to another disbeliever. He has photographic proof. The camel stands by the farmhouse, tethered to a tree. In the foreground, Massey grins and points to the dateline of a newspaper. It's too small to see. Not that it matters, the bet was never time-limited or date-specific.

'There'll be no camel, Graeme said,' Massey tells the disbeliever. 'Fifty quid he bet me that it was a hoax.'

'Aye,' I nod, set up his Guinness and take one of the notes back from him. 'I did think that.'

The bar settles back towards silence, although Massey is aware that he's getting glances. The tugging of his hair, tonight, is less violent – more preening than pulling. As if he's preparing himself for a portrait-painting by Rebecca. He keeps smiling across the pumps at me as if he can't quite believe my stupidity.

'You said, Graeme – ' he begins.

'So, who was it?' I interrupt.

'Eh?'

'Who was it that traded you the camel?'

He shrugs. 'Little fella.'

'Dark complexioned?'

He shrugs again.

'How little?' I persist. 'Like, would he struggle to climb up onto that bar stool beside you?'

'Aye, perhaps.'

I nod, part-satisfied. Maybe that explains how he came to be selling the camel. He'd tried riding it, but ended up clinging to the long neck, unable to grip with his short legs. Perhaps he'd even imagined that the camel's pulled faces and flapping lips were signs of mockery or exasperation. It might explain how he came to be selling the camel, but it didn't explain how he'd come by it.

'And what was he doing with a camel in the first place, then?'

'Never asked.'

'You never asked?'

'No.'

Massey blinks at me. It hadn't occurred to him to be curious. He's let this wee lad bounce off in his Land Rover without, as the saying goes, even looking the camel in the mouth.

'How's he settling into the farm, then?' I ask. 'Are the pigs jealous?'

'He eats hunners,' Massey says. 'But your fifty quid will help towards that.'

'And are you putting him to work?'

A shake of the head. Massey gulps at his Guinness. There's a wrinkle of worry to his forehead now, but he tries to smooth it away with laughter.

'Tell you the truth, Graeme, I'm not too sure what to do with him.'

'Aye, I'd say not.' I pause. 'One humped, I see.'

'Aye, does it make a difference?'

'I'd say not.'

The bar has been busier tonight. With folk wanting to see the photograph of Massey with the camel. Most of them ask follow-up questions, though: how the camel came to these shores; if it can cope with the cold of a Scottish winter; if it spits at the sheep in the fields. And the numpty can't answer these questions, because he didn't ask them in the first place.

'You'll need a plan for it, Massey,' I say.

'For the camel?'

'Aye.' I pour myself a wee nip of whisky, though I'd normally avoid it on a weeknight. 'Don't tell the wife – ' I say. Though I could have can-can girls parading through the bar, pausing mid-kick for me to snort cocaine off their outstretched legs, and she'd probably fail to notice. She'd probably paint it as a forest scene – snow on top of branches.

'It's a scrawny specimen,' Massey says.

'What did the last owner do with it?'

He shrugs.

'Was he...' I consider. 'Of the East, this gentleman?'

'Short fella,' Massey repeats.

'What was his name?'

'Why, you interested in getting yourself a camel too?'

'Let's say I am.'

'Mr Dro-med-ary,' he says, slowly.

'Dromedary,' I repeat. 'Where would that be from?'

'Accent was from down Lancashire way, I'd say.'

'First name?'

Massey shrugs, shakes his head.

It's a week later that Massey calls on Cleland for help. They meet in the bar and Massey buys Cleland a pint from the dregs of the guest ale keg. I'll need to get a new one for next week – I've heard good things about that start-up microbrewery in Dumfriesshire.

'How's he treating you?' Cleland asks. 'The camel.'

'Not well,' Massey frowns at his second Guinness.

'Have you named him?'

A shake of the head.

'A camel needs a name,' I chime in.

'I can't keep him,' Massey says.

'Ah, maybe he doesn't need a name then.'

We all keep schtum for a moment. For Massey, it deepens the worry-line across his forehead. For myself and Cleland, it allows a shared smile and just the first crease of laughter at our cheeks.

'He's stripped the flowerbeds,' Massey says. 'The lawn is down to the roots and he even chews at the jaggy nettles at the side of the driveway.'

'Have you not been feeding him?' I ask.

'I have,' Massey nods. 'He's eaten me out of pig-feed and I think he's even been at the midden. He must have an instinct to stock up on food – for winter or whatever. He has a bottomless stomach.'

'Needs to fill his hump, maybe,' I say.

'Don't we all,' Cleland says. He smiles as he takes a sip of his pint. 'The poor thing's probably just bored, needs something to do.'

'Depressed even,' I agree.

'This is all your fault anyway,' Massey stabs a finger at Cleland. 'You're the one who told me that I should swap the Land Rover for the useless shite.'

'I said no such thing, pal,' Cleland is all innocence now. 'You asked for a valuation and there I was to give you one.'

'Well, I'm ready to sell.'

'Good to hear.'

'I want my seven grand.'

'I'm sure you do.'

They look at one another. Massey seems to have this expectation that Cleland is carrying the money in his back pocket. I wouldn't be surprised if the camel is tied up outside – beside the Toyotas and the Vauxhalls – ready for the trade.

'You think I'm going to sell him for you?' Cleland asks.

'Aye.'

'What makes you think – ' he takes a drink. 'How would I even – '

'You're the one quoted me seven grand for the thing.'

'I'll make a few calls,' Cleland says, regaining his composure. 'But I'll want a commission, like.'

'Get to fuck.'

'Twenty percent.'

'Get. To. Fuck.'

Massey's voice is rising, both in volume and pitch. Other customers are starting to look around. Even Rebecca seems to have stopped, mid-stroke. It's the faintest noise from her – like the whisper of a cough – that causes Massey to sigh, close his eyes, and reconsider.

'Five percent,' he says. 'Only if you get me my seven grand, mind.'

'Ten percent. Whatever the price.'

Cleland hooks his phone from his pocket even before Massey bows his head in acceptance. The younger man makes his way outside. Massey is left at the bar, scrapping his fingers through his hair with enough force to leave a dusting of dandruff beside his empty pint glass.

'Another Guinness, Mass?'

'Ta, Graeme.'

He watches me as I pour the pint. There's an air of desperation about him now. When I set the glass in front of him, he immediately picks it up and slurps the head from it.

'Would you like the camel, Graeme?' he asks.

'What would I want a camel for?'

'I'd give you it at cost. Three grand only.'

'What would I tell the wife. She'd have a – '

I stop. Maybe a new arrival in the lounge area would drag her away from her painting. A conversation piece. There's only so long you can go for without speaking to your spouse, after all. This purchase – four days after her last word – might just force her to confront the camel in the room.

'Not for me, Massey,' I say. 'Sorry.'

Cleland comes back in. He straightens his shirt collar, his cuffs, then perches himself three seats up from where he was before. Leaving a buffer-zone between him and Massey.

'Give us a Tennent's, Graeme,' he says. 'That guest ale tastes shocking. Like it's got a copper-coin at the bottom of it.'

I start to pour out his pint. Massey hasn't stopped staring at him since he came back in. Slowly, as if to embrace the space between them, Massey opens his arms out to Cleland.

'Well?' he asks.

'Eh?' Cleland plays the daft-laddie.

'Do you have someone interested?'

'In the camel?' Cleland purses his lips. 'No.'

'What about your friend in Dubai?'

'I spoke to him, aye. And I sent him your photo of it.'

'And?'

'That was the price for a *premium* camel in *Dubai*. You've got a scrawny shite in Scotland, Massey. Sorry to say.'

'But, what about the seven grand?'

'Aye,' Cleland shrugs. 'You might get two for it, he said. In Dubai.'

'You said seven.'

'But with shipping and that...'

Massey isn't a violent man. Cleland's luck is in on that score. The pig-farmer is the type to make a fist to punch a wall rather than to skelp a young schemie. I'm more worried about the harm he'll do himself than the harm he'll do Cleland.

'He said seven grand, didn't he Graeme?' Massey appeals to me.

'He did, Mass.' I lift a glass to polish. 'Although, to be fair, that was a valuation rather than a promise.'

'The goofy-shite can't be worth nothing, though.'

I'm not sure whether he's talking about Cleland or the camel. I stay silent, waiting on developments. Up the other end of the bar, Rebecca has started painting again. She's cocked her head to the side, looking for a new perspective on whatever it is she sees.

'I'm a fair man,' Cleland says, before drinking deep from his pint. 'I have a friend at the abattoir – might that be a solution?'

'What?' Massey takes his head from his hands to look up at him.

'The abattoir.'

'Kill the thing, you mean?'

Cleland nods. 'Feed the meat to your pigs, maybe.'

'I think it's a delicacy in the Middle East,' I say. 'Maybe you could just sell it like you do with your pork.'

Massey looks at us, from one to the other. He has that startled, glazed look you normally only see in hospital wards and waiting rooms. With a muscle-memory movement, he reaches out to tap at the Guinness pump for the fourth time this evening. Then he turns to Cleland and gives him a single nod.

'It'll cost you fifty-quid in abattoir fees, I reckon,' Cleland says. 'Plus fifty again for my trouble.'

'Whatever,' Massey mutters. 'Just...'

'And I'll make a call about the meat too, see if I can get you a good price.'

I wait for the Guinness to settle, watching Massey over the pumps. He tugs and drags at his hair, until I worry about him pulling it out by the roots.

Cleland is over by the fire, on his phone again. The flames reflect in the sheen of his suit.

I lift the pint to finish it off, then take the money from Massey. It seems his regular night, over the past week, has been extended to four pints. So I'm back in the black. More than the financials, though, I've gained a story to tell.

Tonight. Upstairs. With my cheek against the cold pillow. I'll whisper to Rebecca about Massey's week-long ownership of a camel. Let her tell me that that's boring. That nothing ever changes, nothing ever happens. Sigh and roll away at that, Rebecca. And hiss that we should have sold-up long ago.

# Plein Sud

*Carol McKay*

They're parched. They're hungry. Their mouths are clamouring for nectar – ripe gorgeous juiciness – till they won't shut up, so I stick my thumbs in and split the orange without even peeling it, and there, in the middle of all those plump vesicles of voluptuous orange flesh, is a deformed lump in it.

Well, the girls are *urgh*, *argh* as if they've never seen one before, so I give them the whole talk about navel oranges: about babies growing inside, and the outside of the orange looking like a belly button, only it's neat like theirs, not mine, and they laugh – we all laugh – because mine blobs out and won't go back though they're six and four now and really there's no excuse for it.

I shake the juice from my fingers, lick them clean and wipe them on my towel, then lift my plastic glass for a drink, hoping to hide the mild tremor I feel running through me, and once I've swallowed some – three or four long draughts of it – I tell them how babies used to have their outie pressed in by a copper penny held in place with a ribbon of cream-coloured crepe bandage, and Don sneers at me for that. Not in too unkind a way, but with that riding-crop-and-jodhpurs look he uses when I talk about some of the silly things my old Gran told me when I was growing up.

I think I cover it up quite well. It wasn't thoughts of navels and pregnancies that struck me when I first burst open that orange.

The kids eat it and I lie back down again and have a ponder about it all, or sleep, or I think I do. One glass of wine and my head is dizzy. Okay, more than one. The good thing about this place is its *sieste*. I swaddle myself in a cocoon of balminess till the sound of pebbles grinding under Don's feet brings me out of it.

'What?' I ask, performing a shoulder lift my personal trainer would be proud of. Like a laser the sun hones its beam at me.

'The girls have gone to the water.'

It's a game we're playing. 'It *is* the sea-side.'

'Someone should really keep an eye on them.'

Sand-grit in his tone? A teense of resentment? 'You're a pearl, darling,' I say and lie back down again.

Of course, I peep. The children play their game of who'll-sink-first with the inflatable while Don perches on a ledge of the craggy outcrop within easy reach of them, his English language paper outstretched like a parasol. He's one eye on the kids, one on the paper, and his consciousness floats midway between them and another kind of inflatable that bobs and quivers everywhere you look here in the summertime.

Breasts.

I close my eyes. In my mind I compile an inventory of all the ways I could be heading north: over ninety on the motorway, or clacking over the tracks on the stately slide into St Pancras, or spending the night in limbo – should I say Luton – before the early morning flight.

For now though, we're *plein sud* and it looks as if we're going to stay that way. Not that it's so bad, really. Lots of people envy the life we're living.

Commercial break.

Two steps from the Cote d'Azur's glamorous beaches, your exclusive apartment block towers above the rest. Step inside its cool, marbled interiors. Marvel at the fully-appointed *bijou* kitchen where you'll prepare gourmet meals from the finest ingredients fresh from the picturesque market. Shopping? Lunching with friends? Leave the Beemer in the secure underground *parking* while you dine in the air-conditioned mall. Home again, luxury awaits you as you glide into the corner tub and let the jet mousse soothe away your day.

Part Two.

Sunday's Don's day of rest. From Monday morning to Saturday he's busy busy busy, churning out the financial gobbledegook that makes his world go round, in his fine wool Monte Carlo suits and silky ties. For all I know he could be churning out actual bank notes at the rate he gets to spend them. But look at the free time it gives me.

'I miss you, Don,' I pout to him from my pinkie satin nightie. It's Monday morning and he slips his legs into his silvery summer suit trousers and fastens them without making eye contact, steps into his shoes and puts his foot on the edge of the chair. I try again. 'We used to spend so much time together.' He flicks his eyes up then garrottes the lace.

'We all have to make sacrifices,' he proclaims, lowering over me to pin a perfunctory kiss on my cheek. 'See you at seven.'

Twelve hours of emptiness; the bottle looms large. I pad out of bed, push open the shutters to let the light in then follow him. In the lounge Don lifts a sheaf of papers and his case. 'Bye,' he says and leaves me with the solace of the other cheek kissed. He closes the door and doesn't look back. I do the x-ray trick with the back of the door, imagining him crossing the Greek key floor tiles heading for the elevator. Hear its hum and its carpeted ting.

The lounge is dull: the shutters are still closed. The room is lit only by the down-lights in the scullery that purports to be a kitchen. Open plan. I flick them off and stumble to the windows, throw back the shutters and cross on to the balcony. The air is cooler after the night: less heavy somehow, and the sun doesn't staple you to the planet. I should wake the girls for school. I should shower. I should stutter myself forward into this new day. In my satin nightie I shiver. Wide grey shadows fall over the ground between the apartment blocks. I wrap my arms round my waist, the hairs standing out at an angle; the goose bumps rise high enough to grate with. Don is in the underground car-park. I'll hear the curious squeal as the barrier rises. He'll nod to the concierge and power out, his Saab leaping up the tarmac crest, and then he'll be gone. I lift my eyes. The sea is a panel of stainless steel sheen and the sky's not yet blue. My hand curves on my loose left breast and my fingers know already where to go.

Jingle.

*Life's a giddy whirl, yes it is, when you're a girl.*
*You put on your frock and off you go to dance.*
*With a twinkle in his eye and a vodka, rum or rye*
*He'll have your knickers round your knees if he's a chance.*
*But he wouldn't care a hump if you found a little lump*
*And you can't destroy the idyll here in France.*
*So the moral of the fable is to drink under the table*
*And forget about your fairytale romance.*

Part Three.

When I wake next day there's something rumbling in the background. It isn't me; I'm not quite that hung-over. This is external. But the light is up: my eyes are telling me that, and the bed's cold. I look at the clock. 8.15am. The bedroom is white, white, white. Frighteningly white. The shutters are already open: the rumbling is the construction work to the right of our view. I sit up. The strap of my nightie has slithered down during the night and my left breast pokes its head out to see the world; I lift my bottom, pull up the fabric and scoop my breast back in. My mouth is thick with catarrh. I spit green phlegm on a tissue and hide it under the pillow again. God, I feel rough. Someone is trying to draw a cheese-wire through my brain from back to front. I'm late: the kids will be *en retard* for school. Don has obviously left for work and left me to it – note to self, you must have been unbearable last night – but no matter how rough I feel and how late and inconvenient things are, my left breast still tries to monopolise my attention and I can see it, children's TV animation style, one of two puppets popping its head from a sack, yelling, 'Hello! Hello! It's time to get me checked!'

It's the sheep's *crotte* of nightmares. That's what it is. It's getting so I don't know whether I'm dreaming, or day-dreaming, or whether this monotone white is the walls of a hospital room or my own sweet home-sweet-home.

The girls!

I swallow three paracetamol with a couple of glugs of last night's *Vin de Vin*, grimace then gurgle at the shock, then shake the kiddies from their flushed-cheek-innocence. Another day commences at Pendule Towers.

And another. And a

Part Four.

Done it!

I've arranged with Maggie that we meet for lunch.

I'm not quite sure how I've reached this point. I know that, yet again, the girls arrived at school à point then I drowned my eyes in hot streaming water for longer than a fortnight's worth of showers, and then I think I must have fallen asleep. Let's say, I woke up semi-naked splaying half across the king-size, my nose where Don's neatly folded green checked jimjams peek out from under his hypo-allergenic pillows. The cheese-wire was gone. I think I was still left with some brain. Enough to text Maggie with the words, 'Meet me. *Midi.*' Maggie will know what to do.

I'm early. I will behave. I order orange juice while I wait for her. A thin waiter brings it in a dangerously tall glass, perilously waving his tray in his weak left hand while he sets out napkin, *l'addition* and coaster. He raises a brow and gives a sideways nod as he sets down the juice, not fooled by my foray into liquid that has a zero ethanol composition.

It's *midi* five and she's not arrived. Hasn't even replied. Shit. I was bad to her last time. Sarcasm in a mask. I pick up my glass. The juice is a ball-pool of globules of orange flesh. I suck, and lumps slither up the thick straw onto my tongue. The memory from Sunday comes back to me: the memory of the orange with the lump in it. Finger memory and decorum vie for control of my right hand. I'm compelled to palpate my left breast but clamp my fingers round the chill tall glass, condensation gluing it to my palm. Maggie! I need to tell somebody. Maggie will be the one. But she still hasn't replied. A woman with oversize copper-coloured udders at the table next to me is toying with a rather attractive *pichet de vin rouge*. My mobile sounds. I throw off a prima donna sigh and click my raised thumb and finger. The waiter hates me for it, but Maggie can't come. She has a prior engagement. *Un rendezvous* Scooby-doo. I order my five-a-day in fruit cocktails. Ethanol *de rigueur*.

A boat is skid-bump, skid-bump, skid-bump grinding over the Mediterranean Sea. It's white; far out; I can't make out more than its polygonal shape – wait! Hexagonal – out there on the blue cusp of the waves. I'm watching it. I'm watching it. I'm wishing I was on it and then – flap – my cheek traps shoe-grit on the ground.

This might give me a different angle on things.

Yesterday, I tried to have a serious word with Don, but he wasn't having it. 'Don,' I said. The children were in bed, the dishes were in the dishwasher, the coffee machine was primed and so was my thinking. 'Don,' there's something we need to talk about.'

He was screwing his eyes. Well, he was probably screwing more than one of his interns, but that wasn't the issue.

I waved my right arm, charged with its glass half-full. 'Don. Let me sit here beside you so I can tell you about it.'

I flumped on our cream leather sofa. My knees looked tanned. Darker skinned than the poor cow I was sitting on. My white skirt had ridden up. I tugged at it, left handedly.

'Careful,' Don said, and constructed a barrier of financial newspapers between us.

'Have a drink,' I said, offering my glass. 'Go on! Drink! I want to talk. Us to talk. Two way. Not just you ignoring me.' I thrust my wine towards his mouth.

He directed it away, black hairs thickening near his wrist with its glistening gold Raymond Weil ticker. 'I don't want it, Lynne. And you've had enough.'

I crossed my legs, my slim, tanned, elegant pins, one knee over the other. White skirt half-way up my thighs. It always used to make him come to heel. Not now. 'Don. Don! I need to talk to you. *With* you.' I raised my right arm, glass half-filled still gripped, and tried to wrap it round his – Don, Don; sweet, dear Don. 'Please?'

He leapt. My wine – chilled, *Vin de Vin de* – soaked into his crisp white Chardonnay shirt and the glass smashed – ksshh! – on the marble floor.

Part Five. Historical melodrama.

I'm on a train. The carriage is dark. My father is dark. My grandfather's dark. The sky is dark though it's day. Our cases are dark and the whole city is dark, but we're travelling north towards Mum. It'll be radiant there. I'll cuddle against her breasts where she is soft like pillows. In my head, I cuddle against her breasts and smell her jar-of-cold-cream scent, and she wraps her arms around me even though the train is going *shoong-a-dee-doom, something is wrong.*

My father's in a new black suit with a twin-track ridge that runs over his knees towards the floor. Granddad's tie is black and broad; Daddy's is black and narrow. On the map at school, North points up, and Gran points to Mum there, too.

Part – crazy.

I have a physical disfigurement. It's just a grazed cheek, and it won't last, but here in the school playground I've given the mothers' and nannies' inclination to stare at me new legitimacy. The café people have patched me up with a fine white dressing and my sunglasses go part of the way to obscuring the rest. *Les filles* are terribly solicitous. This grieves me. It isn't my intention to make myself a focal point like this. Maybe I should abandon thoughts of getting myself checked. Maybe I should catch that final train heading north. An everlasting rendezvous with my mother. But I want...! I want...! Doesn't get. I can't do that to my children. I hug them both tight against me.

Don is angry. He's seething with it. I lay off the *Vin de* for the rest of the evening. I even lay off it the following morning. I see the girls to school and help *la Maghrébine* the cleaning lady with the housework. At night, shrivelled like a desiccated sponge inside, I perform my wifely duty, slipping my right hand inside the elastic of Don's green jimjams to find his flaccid penis. He stiffens. Well, the rest of him does. He resists. But he doesn't protest. With my left hand I push the sheet down then sit up. A diffuse light illumines the room and I see the tones of pale and dark where his chest and arms are obscured or catch the light. He's looking at me. It's a game we play. He likes me to wear lipstick for this, and I've applied it painstakingly on account of the tremors. I *frotte* the shaft: thumb, index, middle and ring finger. His breathing lengthens, deepens. He breathes through his nose. I touch my tongue to my lips, bend to suck. Bounce back.

'Don't touch my breast!'

'What the fuck?'

'Don't touch my ...' *Vin de Vin de Vin... Devine.* I leap from the bed. *'Devine! Devine!'*

That's it. He's had it. He's staring from the bed to where I'm scrunched on the edge of it. He's reaching for his slippers. He's going to leave me – go through to the lounge and leave me on my own with it: this gulf between us, like two rigid apartment blocks with shadows in between.

'What the fuck is wrong with you?' he growls again.

'I've tried to tell you.' *Devine! Devine!* 'Can't you guess?'

He's standing, now. Fed up of games. He's turning his back on me.

'Remember my mother?'

He twists his neck to glare at me, brows screwed, eyes hiding in shadow. 'I never met your mother.' He ties the belt of his wrap around his waist.

'I know,' I say, following him to the lounge, my pinkie satin nightie held out on the points of my nipples. The proper defining features. 'She died when I was Jilly's age.' Shuddering – chilled with fright more than low temperature – I clutch my arms around my breasts and stand shivering in front of him.

'This is hardly the time to talk about your mother,' he says, pouring himself gin in two thick fingers.

It is! It is!

My eyes eat up the fruit bowl. The down-light highlights the oranges. Bright roundnesses. Segmented perfection. I choose one; stick my thumbs in and split it without even peeling, and there, in the middle of all those plump vesicles of voluptuous orange flesh, there's a deformed lump in it.

# Bingo Wings

*Vicki Jarrett*

'Bar doesn't open till six, love. You may as well have a seat.' The barmaid with the yellow hair was blunt but not unfriendly.

'That's okay, I'll just wait here, thanks.' Dora knew, as soon as the shutters clattered up and crashed out of sight, there'd be a stampede for the bar. Some of these old dears might look sweet but they'd elbow you right in the tits to get in front.

She shifted her weight from one foot to the other in her queue of one and wondered about the mice. Everyone knew fine the place was infested. She didn't mind sharing, as long as the cheeky wee bastards stayed out of sight till the bingo was finished.

'Come on, ladies. Time you opened up. You've a customer waiting.' Colin sidled up to Dora. He was a little ferret of a man with spots on the back of his neck that glistened under the lights like boiled sweets. 'Got all your books, Doreen? I think you might get lucky tonight!' He nudged Dora theatrically in the ribs and winked. 'I have Caller's Intuition.'

'Oh aye?' Dora raised her eyebrows at him. 'Better make sure and call my numbers then.'

'For you, gorgeous? Anything.'

She was more than twice his age. It wasn't as if she minded that fact, but pretending like she was still a young thing? Some of the other old biddies loved it though, got all giggly and excited. She busied herself rummaging in her handbag. Colin went off to look for a more receptive audience and the shutters rattled up.

Up in the balcony, the usual crew were installed at their table. Dora laid down the tray with their order of drinks and crisps.

'Nice one, Dora,' said Jim, taking a deep pull on his pint and sitting back in his chair. He'd get himself a sly whisky at the bar later when it was his round and Mary would pretend to be none the wiser. Mary and Jim were good at being married. They had a natural ability, the way some folk were good at singing or dancing. It was a gift. The way they accommodated each other reminded Dora of a kind of an old fashioned waltz, each of them anticipating the other's moves. There was a grace about them that couldn't be hidden by any amount of brown cardigans or puffy ankles.

Alec was there too. Mary and Jim's grown-up son wasn't quite all there in the head. Poor soul. His lips were always wet and his clothes, although clean, looked like they'd been corkscrewed onto his body. Sometimes he would get agitated and start shouting and Mary had to miss her game to take him out of the hall until he calmed down. A lot of folk tutted at her for even bringing him. But what was she supposed to do? He might be a grown man, but she couldn't leave him on his own at home.

Dora handed Alec his lemonade and watched as he settled to sucking on his straw, eyes slightly out of focus, completely contented, like a baby with a bottle.

'Has she phoned then?' asked Mary, through a mouthful of cheese & onion crisps.

'No, not this week. She'll be busy. The time difference, and her working shifts, it's hard for her to find a good time. Doesn't want to wake me up in the wee hours just for a chat.' Angela was a nurse and worked hard at it. She'd always been a caring girl, always wanted to help others. Dora pictured her cycling to work in the Australian sunshine, barbecuing dinner on the beach, poised on a surfboard at the crest of a wave, her black hair streaming out behind her like a banner. No wonder she didn't have time to phone. Dora understood. Like the song said, if you loved someone, set them free.

She poured half of her bottle of stout into a glass, arranged her books on the table and tested her dabber on a scrap of paper, making a trail of red dots.

The first games of the night passed without so much as a line for any of them. Dora waved away Jim's protestations that it was his round and hurried back down to the bar, eager to beat the break-time rush. She felt restless this evening and wanted to be doing something. She passed Jim in the press of the crowd streaming down the stairs on her way back up, no doubt using a pretend trip to the toilet as cover for his quick whisky. At the table, Mary was trying to pacify Alec who'd got himself in a bit of a state. He was hunched over, making a mournful keening sound that made something clench and twist in Dora's chest.

'I'll just take him for a walk around the bandits,' said Mary. She chivvied Alec, who was a good foot taller than her, out from his seat and led him by the elbow towards the stairs.

Dora sat on her own and looked out over what had once been a dance floor, back before everyone had televisions and computers to keep them busy. There had been a revolving stage on a massive turntable at the far end. When one band finished their set, the whole thing would revolve, and a fresh band would strike up the next number as they swung into view. Non-stop dancing. That was the Palais' claim to fame and a lot of folk took to it like it was an order, staying on the floor for hours, sweating and spinning till they couldn't walk or think in a straight line.

The polished boards were now covered by a greasy carpet with a geometric design, the space filled with rows of Formica tables and chairs, all kept in their place by thick metal bolts through the legs into the floor. Near the ceiling, the old chandeliers and mirror balls that used to spill a confetti of light over the dancers below, had been replaced with blank white globes, like dead planets. Life had moved on.

The memories this place sprung on her at times disconnected her from the here and now, as if time itself was some kind of puzzle she'd never be able to solve without going mad. All the same, being at the bingo was still better than sitting at home, waiting for nothing to happen. It always did. Then that nothing would become a something – an emptiness that pressed in on her, making her heart race and her hands shake. That was when the other, darker thoughts would creep out of the corners and torment her with detail.

The lights dimmed as Colin again climbed the steps to the caller's raised podium. The chatter died down. People coughed and shifted their feet in nervy anticipation.

Saturday nights were serious money, the sort of money that could change a person's life, if you wanted it changing. Their club linked up with a dozen others across the country and all the prize money was pooled, so your chances of success were much lower but if you did win, the jackpot was far bigger than on an ordinary night. Enough to take a good long holiday in Australia, as Mary had pointed out more than once. Like Dora hadn't worked that out for herself.

The silence stretched tight as all heads turned towards the podium. Colin was obviously savouring his moment as everyone hung on the very edge of his silence. He delivered his line with gravity. 'Eyes down for the National Game.'

The electronic board mounted on the wall at the far end of the hall lit up in a simulated star burst which dissolved to reveal a grid within which the lucky numbers would be illuminated as they were called.

'Sixteen. One and six, sixteen.'

She scanned her card for the number. *Never Been Kissed.* Colin was under orders from club HQ not to use the lingo. More games could be played each session without the frills. But Dora remembered them all, whether she wanted to or not.

She remembered walking into the Palais de Danse on her sixteenth birthday. Like stepping inside a giant hollowed-out wedding cake at Christmas – all creamy columns and layered balconies decorated with pink and white mouldings, the edges trimmed with lights.

Charlie only had a couple of years on her but seemed much older. His swaggering walk, Italian suit, the hank of black hair, heavy with Brylcreem. She knew he got into the fights that broke out in the dark recesses under the balconies where a dangerous current of young men circled like sharks. He would have cuts on his knuckles, maybe a graze on his face, a hint of swelling around his mouth. Somehow this only made his gentleness with her more overpowering. She'd been such an eejit. Never been kissed, right enough. When he dipped his head down to her and spoke softly, rested his hands on her waist, she'd felt a fierce desire to be a damn sight more than kissed. If this was love, it wasn't about hearts or flowers. It was all hot breath and sinew and need.

'Seven and eight, seventy eight.' *Heaven's Gate.*

She'd gone outside for some air. Really she was looking for Charlie.

Outside, the front of the Palais was a large rectangular slab of art deco with thin leaded windows and a triangular gable over four columns. Behind the façade, the hunched barn of the main hall squatted like a shameful secret.

'Dora! Over here.' He was leaning against the side of the building, smoking. His face flared in the glow from the burning tip of his cigarette before falling back into darkness. 'Come on, I've got something to show you.'

Around the back of the building, among the empty crates and rubbish bins, they slid together into a darkened doorway marked Deliveries Only. A hand at the small of her back pulled her in close, another slid under her full skirts. There was a small thud as the back of her head bumped against the metal door.

'Four and one. Forty-one.' *Life's begun.*

Back inside, as they slow danced, her head on his shoulder, breathing in his smell, her limbs seemed not to be joined to her body in the same way. The springs under the dance floor no longer supported her as she moved but seemed to work against her, causing her to lurch and sway, to cling to Charlie. Thinking of the potential consequences made her feel queasy. But everyone knew the first time was safe. They'd be more careful in future.

'Two and eight. Twenty-eight.' *In a state.*

The pain was more than anyone could ever have warned her. It rose up in dark red waves that swamped her completely. 'Pain' was too small and weak a word for this force. It was bigger than her, bigger than the room, the hospital, something separate and unstoppable. Her mother walked over to the window in small precise steps and stared into the darkness with her lips pressed together.

The numbers kept coming and Dora stamped them off one after another. She glanced up at the podium. Soon the game would be over and Colin would be reduced once more to making smutty innuendoes to get attention. He would stay up there all the time if they'd let him, Dora thought.

Her card was filling up as if Colin was reading the numbers over her shoulder. She felt sweat prickle on the back of her neck. Her sense of being on the edge of something increased. She pressed her forearms down hard on the table, trying to get a grip without making it obvious she needed to. It felt as if the whole balcony was tipping forwards into the hall in the direction of the café at the far end, where the revolving stage used to be.

The whole affair had been managed by two hand cranks, one on either side of the stage. 'Watch this,' Charlie had whispered in her ear, then walked that walk of his towards the stage. Dora watched as he and three of his pals took hold of the cranks, two men to each, and started working them as hard as they could. The stage began to turn, slowly at first, then with increasing speed as the Johnny Kildare Orchestra went into the closing bars of 'I'll be Loving You Always'. The band leaned in against the spin, tried their best to look as if nothing was happening, and kept playing. They were half way round when there was a grinding noise and the stage left its runners altogether, tipping the band off into a flailing pile of tuxedoes and instruments. Cheers went up from the crowd. Charlie and his mates sped past, an irate brass section close behind.

'One and three. Thirteen.' *Unlucky for some.*

There was no reason to think Angela *wasn't* nursing in Australia. No reason at all. Certainly no reason to imagine she'd ended up a druggie, like those lassies in the flats, shacked up with some arsehole who beat her up, or with ten kids she couldn't feed that got taken off her one by one by the social, or giving hand-jobs to men who avoided eye contact and swore at her when they came, or beaten and dumped in a ditch with her own bra twisted around her neck, eyes wide open, staring at the sky for days, weeks, without anybody noticing she was gone. And all of it made possible because she believed her own mother didn't want her, had never loved her. But that wasn't true at all.

What was true and what wasn't didn't make much difference to what happened to a person in life. It hadn't to her, or to Angela – if that was even her name now, wherever she was, whoever she was. Adoption was easily done in those days. Happened all the time – the product of ignorance and prejudice. She wasn't anything special. She just thought too much. That'd always been her problem. Left to her own devices, her mind invariably wandered back to the well-worn track of whatever happened to her girl. Hoping everything worked out for her, hoping she had a good life, hoping she didn't think too badly of her. Hope was a bastard, but it was also the only thing she had that couldn't be taken off her. It was both her escape and her prison; life support and life sentence. It pulled her through the years, days, seconds, gifting and cursing her from breath to breath with a string of empty promises. Without it she'd hardly be human.

There was a sudden eruption of activity right at the back of the balcony. A woman with wispy white hair and enormous glasses shouted and leapt out of her seat, squawking and flapping.

'We have a claim!' announced Colin.

A uniformed girl came running to check the woman's card. The microphone buzzing in her hand.

'I need to see your card.'

'But I've not won!' shouted the woman who by now looked as if she was about to take off. 'Look – there!' She pointed towards the shadows in the corner behind her seat. 'Mouse, you stupid girl! Not house – *mouse*! See? Over there by the wall. Bold as brass, looking at me like it owns the bloody place.'

Dora stood and peered in the direction the woman was pointing and, right enough, there sat a small brown mouse, perfectly still, its black eyes glinting. Calmly, as if pleased it had made its point, it turned and padded out of sight.

The hall was in an uproar, some were laughing, some shouting abuse at the woman for interrupting the game. Colin kept repeating, 'Can I have the code number please?'

Eventually the girl shouted over her mic, 'No claim!' and the game continued.

'Three and one. Thirty one.' *Get up and run.*

Full house. Couldn't be. But it was.

Alec was watching her, a droplet of spit slowly descending from his lower lip. Without looking up from her game, Mary reached over with a tissue and wiped it away before tucking the tissue into the sleeve of her cardigan.

Dora felt a falling, draining sensation that left the top of her head buzzing with cold, her ears filled with sea-shell emptiness. This wasn't supposed to happen to her. She looked at Mary and Jim, at the rows of heads in the hall below, bowed over their cards.

Then the realisation. She didn't have to say a thing. If she simply waited, someone else's card would fill up. Just a matter of time. All she needed to do was wait.

Colin's intercom crackled into life carrying the distant shouts of a winning claim in one of the other halls. Dora twisted her card tight and pushed it firmly into the neck of her almost empty bottle.

Mary and Jim were comparing their missed numbers, groaning and laughing over their near misses. Mary looked up at her, 'No luck either then, Dora?'

Dora felt light, as if she could launch herself off the balcony and fly in great swooping arcs around the hall. 'No, not tonight, Mary. Maybe next time.'

'We live in hope eh?' said Jim, rising from his seat and gathering up the empty glasses. 'Same again?'

# Oona

*Eleanor Thom*

We liked the shape of her, the way it felt to write her down, the smooth circles inked on scraps of paper as we sat up late, throwing names between us like a game of tennis. And then she was born and the name matched. Her face was round, and her lips were full. I held her against my skin, the circles of my dark nipples and the circles of her cheeks. She had arrived late and I was ready to feed her, but when she didn't open her mouth the midwives took her away. They said she was going to be warmed up. They swaddled her like a sausage roll and sat her upright on their knees. They clapped her on the back while she pulled angry faces and gurgled and blew spit bubbles. It was normal, the midwives said, and we trusted them and waited for her to be ready. Birth was a shock to a baby, after all.

Only later, when her mouth still wouldn't open, when the tip of a finger between her lips was met with a gummy bite, then we could tell they were worried.

My son was a milky baby. That was his word for them, 'milkies', or sometimes he called them 'milky side' and 'other side'. We never knew which breast was which. We thought it might change depending on which nipple was more giving. He was nearly three years old before he dropped his last feed, the one that got him up in the morning, his equivalent of my strong coffee. They say that breastfeeding is an unreliable contraceptive, but it must have been working for us, because within a few months of stopping we found out that his sister was coming. We took our son to see her on an ultrasound, a 3D scan that showed us how alike they were going to be. Her features blurred and smudged, but occasionally they came into focus. The images had a golden hue.

'She's a popcorn baby,' said her big brother.

Not long after that, lying in bed one morning, our son told me that the popcorn baby would be a bottle baby, not a milky baby. My milkies belonged to him, he said. No, I told him. The sister would also be a milky baby, but he would be able to cuddle me while she fed. It would be a nice time for us all.

'Okay,' he agreed. 'She can have one of them. We'll have one each.'

I tried to imagine us all in the bed, the whole family, four of us together, but somehow I found it hard. I worried about the amount of space in the bed, but not about breastfeeding. It would be easier with a second baby. The first time was hard. I remembered the burning pain each time my son latched, gritting my teeth and stamping my feet on the floor to stop myself from screaming. My nipples bled and wouldn't heal, and my breasts suddenly felt like new worlds, violent places that were evolving. Inside me there were channels forming, trickling streams, ducts. It was a whole new ecosystem, a milk age. I smothered them in ointments and wrapped them in gauze. I rang the helpline while sobbing and wiping snot off my face. Everything was uncomfortable. My caesarean stitches itched. My knees were sore from kneeling on the carpet to change his nappies. The pain was cutting and I was exhausted, but my mother had fed me, and I was going to feed this baby myself if it was the last thing I ever did. No one and nothing was going to damn well stop me.

And then it got easier. He was big to begin with, and he drank everything I could make and he fattened quickly, a seal pup. A rugby ball. We laughed as we tried to count his chins.

If he slept well, which wasn't often, I would run a bath. I looked at my body under the water, the unfamiliar lolloping bits and sinking depressions. The sternum, a weird lump of bone protruding just below my ribs. I'd never noticed it before, but now it seemed to hold up everything below it, like the pole in the middle of a marquee. The pigmentation gathered in my belly button, a murky inkwell, and around it my tummy was soft and tender, uncontained. When I pressed my fingers in I felt the contours of the bits beneath, as if my organs were jumbled loosely in a plastic bag. The wound was numb. A cold, tingling sensation was all I got there.

The warm bath brought out the milk. It gathered over me like clouds, like when you put a dash of milk into your tea and it swirls and spreads.

When Chris kissed my body in bed, the milk leaked into his mouth. He pulled a face. Melon juice is how he described the taste. Melon juice and something else, more human and more bodily. He wrote an email to a friend describing the taste in detail. The friend was another dad, but in a sleepy confusion, Chris fired off the message to the wrong person. It was a musician he'd worked with. The musician was getting well known and his face was often seen in the Sunday Arts supplements. He didn't reply. Sometimes I still imagine him playing his guitar and thinking about that misdirected message, the secret it contained. Milk and melon juice. We had a good laugh about that.

We soon learned that we could use the milk for all sorts of things. It healed cuts, disinfected crusty eyes, and took the heat out of a rash overnight. I'd heard of breast milk shrinking cancers in laboratory Petri dishes and I could believe it. The stuff seemed miraculous. My friend, Morag, was donating. They had places called milk banks.

Morag was my first mummy friend. We met before the babies were born at an aqua-natal class at the local pool. Chris had come to watch from the gallery a few times. He said I'd have gotten more exercise sitting on the sofa and stroking the cat. This was true. Us pregnant mothers floated around on foam sausages, enjoying the temporary weight off our feet, and chatting. A water-café for hippos, Chris said.

Morag had beautiful long hair and she was the kind of person who did good things, who would find the time to cook properly with actual ingredients, who would buy quality bras, and attractive shoes, and then she could still laugh when her daughter leaned over to be sick on them. And this goodness was overflowing because when it came to milk, Morag was an over-producer. Her finely supported bosoms could feed the four thousand. And so she expressed the surplus milk, and once a week it was collected by a man who arrived on a motorbike. He took away the frozen milk and delivered it to the milk bank. The milk bank. I imagined the place, an icy vault lined with shelves, a room that contained the power to save the tiniest, earliest babies, the ones that take their mothers' bodies completely by surprise. I thought of this gifted potion, the thousands of miniature milk bottles. Glass ones with silver foil lids, like the bottles the milk man used to deliver to the doorstep of my childhood home. That's what a milk bank looked like in my mind.

At some point I bought a breast pump, a strange octopus of a thing with tentacles and flanges, and multiple parts. It had to be connected in the right way, then unconnected and sterilised before they could be put back together and reused. It looked like a lot of bother. I plugged it in and sat with it sucking at me. I felt irritated by it and collected a dribble. Our son felt different to the pump. When he suckled, at first it felt like a dog's nose rubbing against your hand, wet and excited. Then the milk started to flow, and I'd feel it draining out of me like a valve had been turned. I'd hear his long, slow gulps, till finally he'd close his eyes, and half asleep, he'd suck gently, a fluttering sensation. At the end of a feed my breasts felt saggy. They felt like my purse does after throwing out the detritus, all the stuff that accumulates there over time: receipts, train tickets, folded up notes on scrap bits of paper, and loyalty cards for shops and cafes that I probably won't visit again. Disappointed that the pump hadn't done its job, I put the thing away. I wasn't going to try again.

Oona was two days old. Her mouth was still full of bubbles, still clamped shut, and by then we knew she was struggling. I sat with a midwife, my gown open, pinching myself with a thumb and fingertip to express the sticky droplets that come before the milk. Colostrum is as yellow as Birds custard powder, the paste you make before you add the remainder of the pint. It is breast milk concentrate, the ultimate medicine. Ounce by ounce, colostrum is more valuable than gold, and my fingers were wet with it. The midwife held a syringe and as each bead of the precious liquid appeared she tried to suck it into the nozzle. It was ridiculous, and painstaking. I was reminded of the litters of rabbits we'd bred years ago. Sometimes they came out not right, too small, or one eyed, or an odd shape, but we always tried to save them. We crushed Weetabix biscuits into milk and slowly, very gently, we fed them by hand. We willed their tiny mouths to open for the food. Sometimes they lived. Sometimes not. Sometimes you expected them to die and then they surprised you.

The doctor was examining Oona. On the bed in front of us he pulled at Oona's limbs like a raw chicken. Her face contorted. Her legs were sensitive. They hung limp from her body, her little right foot curling upwards and inwards.

'Her lip is a bit strange when she cries,' he said, pulling hard again on her legs. When he spoke I noticed his tongue through a gap in his teeth, and I got an odd feeling that he was suppressing a smile.

'Have you noticed,' the doctor said. 'She looks like Elvis.'

He wasn't so perfect either, I thought. He had a lisp, very slight but it was there. I wanted to ask him to leave.

'There are some tests,' he said. I heard the lisp again. I heard this and other bits of what he was saying. Blood to be sent away. Electric shocks down her legs. Electric shocks! I wouldn't allow that.

'Not now,' he said when I objected. 'But maybe something for the future.'

He wrapped Oona in a blanket and returned her to us.

'Other than that, a perfectly healthy baby,' he said cheerfully, finally releasing the smile that I was sure he'd been holding back. He caught my eye briefly before leaving the room.

I sent everyone away after that. I didn't want to look at anyone but Oona. I sat thinking back to that day when I was lying with my son in the bed. I'd not been able to imagine bringing her home, and I'd dismissed the feeling, worrying instead that the bed we would share was too small.

The hospital breast pumps were big yellow things that whizzed around on wheels. One showed up in my room when Oona was four days old, a pump and a strange tank of water that smelt funny. No one commented on its being there or showed me what to do, but I fiddled with the pump's plastic parts till they fitted together in what seemed like a sensible order, and I put the cups to my chest. It was better than the one I'd had at home. The motor of the home pump had leered at my tits, shouting 'oooh-aaah-oooh-aaah' as it half-heartedly sucked them. This was quieter. And so I tried to do what I'd been told to, relax, think of my baby, believe in myself and in my body. I watched the milk start to appear and I tried not to look at the numbers on the bottles, naught to one hundred printed up the sides like a ladder I had to climb.

By now I had new, medical words in my daily vocabulary that I resented. They had taken Oona into Special Care, and here they used these words all the time, a language I never wanted to learn. 'Mils,' and 'cares' and 'aspirate'. 'Cares' were something they did to her every four hours, reaching hands into the incubator through holes in its side and changing her nappy, wiping the dried secretions off her lips. Milk wasn't called milk here. They called it E.B.M. (expressed breast milk), or Aptimil, and it was administered, not suckled. They delivered it, her 'feed', through a spaghetti-thin tube that had been inserted through a nostril while I was sleeping. No one had asked my permission.

By now I could picture exactly what forty mils looked like. I knew how long it would take for the milk to snake its way down the thread into Oona's tummy, but I wasn't producing enough. What I was able to make was barely enough to wet her lips, so that's what I used it for. It was hard for her to lick, but she tried. I glimpsed her tongue flicking, as if the idea of licking was somewhere there in her mind. We weren't without hope.

The nurses told me not to be hard on myself. Stress affects milk supply. The amount they put down the tube seemed like far too much, but what did I know about formula? It would keep her alive when I wasn't able to fill their measured syringes. I could add all the breastmilk I produced, they said. But my own milk still hadn't come in, just endless dribbles of colostrum.

'Don't feel bad,' they said. So I didn't, but in the back of my mind I was thinking about those motorbikes, the bikers that picked up the frozen milk from Morag's house, and from the houses of other mothers who had milk to give. It was milk for the babies that came too soon and milk for the babies who needed it most. Milk that could buy me some time. A chance to catch up. No one had mentioned a milk bank. Did they have one, I wondered?

I was in a meeting with three doctors. Oona probably had a syndrome, they said. The twisted foot we'd seen clearly on the ultrasound was part of a pattern, low muscle tone, feeding trouble.

'What syndrome?'

They didn't know. The doctor with the lisp did the talking. I'd complained about him and his tone was different this time, but his voice was loud and I didn't buy his concern.

'Oona's condition could get better. Or it could stay the same. Or she could get worse,' he said, speaking slowly as if I was one of his paediatric cases.

Give the man a prize, I thought.

Beside the doctor the orthopaedic specialist fixed her gaze somewhere on the patch of sky outside the window. I thought again about my rabbits, the ones that were born looking wrong. Some of them lived. And some of them didn't. But some of them surprised you.

The third consultant, my obstetrician, shifted uncomfortably in the corner. She only spoke to me when I asked her a question, and she answered briefly and quietly, her thin arms and legs folded, her long fingers neatly clasped on her knee. I was sad to think that this was probably the last time I would see her. She had delivered my son three years earlier, and I had emailed her as soon as I knew I was pregnant for a second time. She was someone we had trusted to slice me open and pull out our babies, and just a few weeks earlier we had re-introduced her to our son. We said 'Look! This is the surgeon who lifted you out into the world, who saved you when you were stuck. These are the hands that first touched you.'

When the meeting ended we all stood up at the same time. I don't remember saying goodbye, or what I did next. I was probably thinking about milk. It was something useful I could do, trying to reach the next rung up the sides of the little bottles. They were little white bottles with numbers from 20 to 100 mils. They were not miniature glass bottles with silver lids. They were nothing like the ones the milk man used to bring. And then at some point later I started to cry in a way that I had never cried before. A midwife and her assistant sat with me, and I don't know if it was dark outside, or if they turned off the lights. I only remember the dark, the sadness in their eyes, the way we all leaned towards each other, the sound of their voices.

I was sitting in my room that looked out over the hospital car park. People were arriving and leaving, visitors with teddies and flowers, people towing pink and blue balloons. Oona was sleeping and I had eaten. I had to eat to make milk, so I ate. I was also playing with my phone, and then I thought I'd take a minute and look it up. The milk bank. I'd write them an email, that's what I'd do, if I could find the contact details. It was worth a shot, I thought. The phone in my hand was fiddly and the connection was almost non-existent, but I persevered. I walked over to the window and held it up to the sky, willing the screen to load. And then it appeared, the lower case 'f' in the corner, the blue banner across the top. I'd found it at the first try. The milk bank was on Facebook.

The phone on the other end of the line was ringing. I imagined the place again, glass bottles on shelves, the chilled, chalky liquids inside them vibrating slightly as the phone rang, insistent.

'Hello?'

It was a woman, a mother. I could hear a child's voice in the background, and the woman turning from the phone to gently shush it away to other things. A mum like me in a house somewhere, with toys, letters on the doormat, dishes piling up, a heap of laundry. A normal house. She ran the page for the milk bank, she said, and I told her Oona's story.

Word must have spread around the hospital. People I didn't know suddenly asked me how I was, calling me over by name as I walked up and down the corridors. 'How is your girl?' they asked. We came and went quietly each day, arriving early in the morning with my milk in a cool bag, milk to top up the formula, milk that I had expressed by hand in the car, hiding my breasts behind the dash board. At home I expressed on the pump they lent me, up in the middle of the night, first thing in the morning, after putting our son to bed, any spare minute I had. One morning I moved too quickly and the pump made a raspberry noise against my breast. It was loud and wet, and Chris woke with a fright.

'What was that?' he shouted.

'My boob,' I laughed.

This was the new way of things. I was getting a little more each time, but every day Oona needed more than she had the day before. Back and forth driving on that road with the milk in the cool bag. Going there in the morning, coming back in the dark, listening to the same album each night. 'What happened to my brother' sang the singer, and I heard it in my head, rewritten.

*What happened to my daughter,*
*Her frightened little eyes,*
*Did something shake her brain on that long bus ride...*

The morning after I phoned the milk bank, we saw the motorbike parked outside the front of the hospital. It had a body like a wasp, and tropical paintwork, orange and luminous yellow in a checkerboard pattern. The mum I had spoken to on the phone had explained the service. The milk was kept in Glasgow and they had a surplus. She told me to ask for it. The milk has a shelf life and they wanted the stock to be used. As soon as it was needed, a motorcyclist would be dispatched with the milk, still frozen, and it would speed down the A77. The driver of the motorbike would be a volunteer. It would be someone who did it for the love of the ride, of revving the bikes, passing by the traffic that clogged the junctions south of Glasgow, helping tiny babies by doing what they loved, by driving. Hell's Angels with breastmilk in the top box.

'Did you ask about the milk bank?' Chris said. He had noticed the bike too.

'Yeah,' I said. 'I asked a nurse.'

'And?'

Chris was great. He had been behind me one hundred per cent, getting through the tough times with our son, when feeding was sore and exhausting.

'She said she didn't know,' I told him. 'She'd have to ask the doctor.'

Chris grunted.

'Ask again,' he said.

We rang the bell of the neonatal unit and waited to be buzzed in. Sometimes they took a while to answer, and while we stood there my nipples started to feel funny, a buzzing, burny feeling. They knew we were getting close to the baby. They call it a let down, which makes it sound like a bad thing, but it's not.

'Do you remember that time I was feeding Ivor on the sofa,' I said, 'and your dad was so distracted he sat on a cake.'

We laughed. My father-in-law liked to see the babies breast fed. He had visited for our son's first birthday party and he'd given me a statue of a woman breastfeeding a young child. The child lay relaxed across her lap.

They buzzed us in.

'Ask again about the milk,' Chris said.

We saw Oona through the glass section of the door. I always looked at her through that small window before I went in, to see if she was awake and waiting for us. Often she would lie studying the motifs we had printed out and taped to the sides of her bed. That morning there was a nurse I'd not met before sitting next to her. She had chin-length blonde hair. We pushed the door open and the nurse looked up and smiled.

'Ah, good. Are you the mum that asked about the donor milk?'

She came over with a form in her hand. 'I've got it all here ready and I've warmed it up. Shall I just give it to her now and you can sign after?'

My eyes felt hot all of a sudden, filling up. That's what the milk feels like inside you once it's flowing. It doesn't want to stop. We can make milk like we can make tears. I was going to cry because I was so relieved. The milk was here. Another mum had saved us. The bike we saw had come for Oona.

'You can relax now,' the nurse said. 'Your own supply will catch up in no time.'

The donor milk was already running into Oona's tube, a ribbon of white. Whatever was wrong, I knew that now she had a better chance. Someone had given us this.

Later I signed the form and I looked at Oona's name printed along the top. When I was pregnant we thought all the O's in her name were like planets. The double 'O' in her first name is mirrored by another double 'O' in her surname. Now I could see that they were like something else, like two sets of boobs.

'Are you okay?' the nurse asked.

I was thinking about the boobs in Oona's name, and I was thinking again about the baby rabbits. Sometimes there was one that was so poorly, you never expected it to live through the night, but you'd get up in the morning and find it scampering round the hutch. Oona was going to be like that. The one that surprised everyone.

That night, when we came home from the hospital, we didn't put our son to bed. Instead we took him to a fun fair. He was three and a half and he had never tasted candyfloss. I wasn't well enough for the rides but I watched as Chris disappeared with our boy through the doorway of the crooked house. What am I doing here? I thought. I was shivering and sore. I watched the bright lights spinning on the rides and pushed my hands into my pockets. It was cold. A few moments later my son emerged. He waved to me from a first floor balcony that was slanted like a quizzical eyebrow. 'What *are* you doing here?' the crooked house's expression seemed to say.

Our son ran towards a gigantic inflatable slide. He kicked off his shoes before I could stop him. It was getting late. I could feel my nipples starting to burn and I knew I was full with milk. How many mils had I managed to make today? How many rungs up the ladder on the side of the bottles? I should have insisted on going home to express the milk, but , my son was having too much fun.

'Just one go,' I said.

In the car park behind us there was a gang of bikers, engines revving, adjusting helmets. The lights of the fairground were reflected in their visors. They started to move forward, getting ready to disappear into the darkness. If they headed east they would zip past the hospital where Oona was sleeping. I hoped she was sleeping.

'I'm climbing up. Watch me!' our son shouted, bouncing off the bottom of the slide, rolling his clumsy body up the first three rungs on the ladder to go again. The steps were huge and wobbly and they kept pushing him down, but he wouldn't give up. The laughter hurt so much I thought my stitches were being ripped right out of my wound. But our boy kept trying to get up that ladder, and eventually, finally, he made it to the top. For a second I felt like I was there with him, right at the top, brimming with it.

# Bad Players

*Roddy Lumsden*

Halfway down the carriage, the cackling girl,
too loud for my introspective sensibilities,
turns out to be a bloke, someone Stoke City
might have let go, free transfer, circa 1980.
I think of the girl swimmer who rouses herself
at 6am, to knock through two hundred lengths,
but behind her back, her nickname is 'Seventh'.
I want to hug those who make the semis, those
who dream on, those who reach county stage,
hit the under 21s then flood away. You triers,
you are okay, even decent, but you do flail
when the proper people nail you. Sorry, losers.
I am nothing much but I go for what I go for
because life has only offered me that much.
At the tail end. The senior circuit. Do you see
hills dipping through mist, dead legs, bullies
tipping something you loved into the lake?
You got to the last stage of the interview?
And now it's a balcony and the glass of wine
and the ciggy, which tastes vile, to the taste
of one who wins. We are quite content
to put 'quarter-finalist' on your headstone,
okay about patting you and saying, softly,
'you did quite well'. Come over, I am open
to talking this with you, I am only part winner,
I have been there in the suburb of all discontent.
My heart has been dubby. I have at times, oh,
at times, screwed. I look at you, bad players,
and think of time I have spent on my own,
the sad walk to hope. And now you are
out for a duck, taken off at half time. Your
Olympic dream remains a dream. Bad player.
Late light on the pitch calls you on and you
and, horror, I are going nowhere and we know
it's over. Heroes, we were something once.

# Towns You Only Pass Through

*Roddy Lumsden*

Their systems linger, awaiting your arrival,
which will not happen. We zip, we air gun,
and we do not stop. Windygates, Kenilworth,
I see your Co-ops, your lonely ironmongeries,
your tangle of lanes I might possibly dally in.
Chesterfield, I doubt we will ever meet proper.
Yet a newsagent sign catches my eye, a woman
bent to some task of thought. On a wet corner
in Barnstaple, a vicar and a poppet bat a balloon.
It is green and always must be. Gary, Indiana,
proving this is everywhere, or some grey town
south of St Malo, where we did not stop to buy
beef for that chilli or a basket of cold beers.
Newark and Stevenage, fetish settlements
for the passer through, each with its microcosm
of neverness, model villages helium pumped
till bachelors and long lost women parade
their shadowier provinces, seeking orange juice
or scourers or the last paper plates in the store.
Make my point? Oh, it is that there is not one.
I grew to what I am in a town you can never
pass through, unless you are driving into the sea.
Passing through is ever a sort of phobia, a fear
that the lethal or panic might happen anywhere
and best to move to destination. Arrival
is always the better of it. You clasp your sides
and stretch, you ready. What would come
is simmering with value, it will tie you
in its maze of desperate but needful inevitability.
Gort, with your Brazilians and your meat;
Salem, Oregon, not even the frightfullest Salem;
Stara Pazova, an instant gush of the 1950s, now.
I will get over you, by which I mean so many things.
I might run through you, crowing 'not for me',
I might mention you in passing, boredly, probably
only to myself. You are not worth the sleep

I might lose. But cannot lose. Northampton, bless,
some lazy morning I will drive through you
in a souped-up Bentley I cannot even drive.
And my dear heart will burst with the awfulness
of reaching your shrubby limits, of carrying on.


# Fear of Lions

*Roddy Lumsden*

*Q: Where does a lion go to sleep?*
*A: Wherever he wants.*


At least I know now that I will never take charge
of the master ship, ploughing the sounds
around an undiscovered continent,
Good Hope unrequited, unrequired,
turning the great wheel with my elbows,
in inch thick blindfold, to give the task
more bustle. No admiral then, no swinging anchor,
more a quaking, melancholy anchorite.
My saintly attributes will be these:
a nightingale clinging to my dowdy epaulette,
a disc-faced owlet, dunked in the bolehole
of my new-sprouted willow. And together
we will battle our fear of lions,
those gaspy boys, those slick girls cantering
through head-high grass, needy
to gift us to their bellies, so the charm of sleep,
the slumberlust, might start

# Split

*Mike Saunders*

The opposite to 'sweet' is 'scratch', not sour, I find
when the bramble splits a future scar into my arm

thin as horse-hair, but
deeper than it should be: panic, unpanic,
running adjacent to an artery, up to my fist.

A split second earlier
                 a blackberry had rested there,
before my hand clutched the shock
and split the cluster of droplets
over fingerprint and thumb.

         Now, there is little difference
         in the translucent wash:
             both red-coloured-red
                 some fruit
                 some flesh
          both skin, both berry.

                  Later, I open the cut
                  to make it speak
                  but it moans, and re-stitches
                  its split lips.

                  I open it again, and finally it whispers:

*with thorns, you really have to lean in*
*to get them out*

# Valencia

*Graham Hardie*

the oranges are black,
like the gypsy heart hanging
from the decaying olive branch—
'sing, sing, sing you mutants,
you reptiles of madness!'
and they sang, the children
of the flying moon, with wings
of hawks and eagles and
the dead birds of Valencia.
the fruits are ripe on
the white sun's blemished breast,
as the gypsy sucks the nipple,
with greed and all man's envy.
the cliff's edge is the corner
of the mouth of the lion's breath,
and it ruminates on the mountain
boat, without sailors or wind,
and where the sails are ripped
by angels carrying jars of gypsy
blood, offered to those lonely
and isolated and who feed on sex.
'scream, scream, like the Devil
in a white coat!' and they screamed
for the end, the end of everything,
in the world of floating enigmas
and apples with fangs of silver,
which pierce the gypsy in his eye
of fortune and stories told!

# Corrugated Iron

*David McKelvie*

Some autumn wave in winter.
Some airbrushed splinter of a sun
setting somewhere behind the grey.
Some day of rust pasted on a curtain
closed and drawn to and floating
for a second, a morning, the day.

These are roofs and walls of use –
beauty is a stranger, no wonder
the rust gathers and paint flakes
in the coolth of the north –
it seems bound by the colour of the rope,
plastic orange, hanging under.

Rust is the colour that shouts
in a landscape of green and speckle
and rust covers the iron; rust is
and has no option but to be the iron
that stands, clacks, creaks and sings
in the wind and watered air.

# A Demonstration

*Craig Coyle*


I reached in through his auditory canal and
plucked out his Pineal Gland.
Ha! He diminished like a punctured balloon...
This puddle on the floor, I said, was once a man,
a Grand Cartesian
who dined, and speculated
of the pneumatics of mind
and muscularity. Look at him now,
a soup with a skin of car salesman smile...vacant.
Step around him, gentlemen, don't wet
your shoes! Another paradigm shift
is due to sweep through.
Farewell. This demonstration was brief
and I am sure to survive you.


# Lab Notes for Vladimir Holan

*Craig Coyle*


I caught a particle of time, a fragment.
Slower than the others, as if one of its wings
was slightly damaged...crippled, perhaps,
by the weight of a memory.
I placed it in a jar. Like a firefly.
When the darkness comes, I take it out.
Sometimes, this is how we sleep. Sometimes, why we hold constant vigil.
But its decay products are simply the blurry passage of even smaller particles of time...
Why is it, that because we love,
things die twice?

# The Witness of St Benedict of Nursia
## *Patron Saint of the Poisoned*

*Andy Jackson*

There wasn't time to breathe, or even think
before I took it, just the bulging of my throat,
the bolus plunging like a broken lift. *Drink
it down, every drop*. I felt it drain and coat

the sump of my stomach, hot as a hasty dram.
Who would choose the other way, the years
of tiny doses, every day another gramme,
grated into casseroles, dissolved in beer

till signs emerge of its accumulation; falling
out of hair, a loosening of teeth, skin the shade
of ash? Some can stomach this slow culling,
this protracted dissolution; some are made

to drain the glass in one, feel it settle cruelly
in their guts, caustic as peroxide, not as swift
as hemlock, but then nothing in this life is truly
colourless, or odourless. A happy end is a lift

you can't refuse, one for the road, a slow boat
home, the dark house at the end of a drive,
where those you love are looking for an antidote,
knowing there can be none, except to be alive.

# Atmospheric

*Rob A Mackenzie*

The hairdressers stopped by to snip
and slice their way through the village,
arranged bouquets of missing children
during scheduled cracks in routine.

Soldiers admired the blades, waved
like stray threads at the women battling
with absence. There was no love for
enemy comb-overs even in darkness.

The soldiers chose clouds and opened
fire. As if cattle, the clouds rattled
sour milk on their mohicans. It seemed
clouds die a slow death, as everyone

resembled them after a while, falling
gradually apart. 'Atmospheric' was how
the anchorman put it. There will always
be work for hairdressers during a war.

# The Low Road
## Manchester 2013

*Stuart A Paterson*


Doon daunerin aside the auld canal,
Ablo the reek an keech that wullnae shift
Aff fae ma claes an stangs an staws ma thrapple,
Ah fin a kina coupit, dingit lift.

A lift that's drapp't, no risen, oot o smogs,
A lift criss-crossit by a million brigs
Doon here whaur sheughs mair regular than clocks
Tuim life an time oot lang-negleckit riggs

Awa fae sicht an mense o thon abuin.
Forby, thur streets are sic that gin ye fa
There's nae wey up or oot, there's ainlie doon
An through an oan whaur gear is nocht ava.

Wha'd bide here? Shedda thirled tae a nicht
O grieshoch fag-end starns, tae clockwork munes
An haun-me-doon deliveries o licht
That doiter freenless, fleeing fae the sun.

Oad-times, the watters swall an loup an chirm
Like ferlie kinna wechts tae pass the boats
Through murkin-driven glaumeries an sclims,
Then draps tae let thaim hirple gledly oot.

Doon daunerin aside the auld canal,
Ah lowse ye, Scotland, fae ma dingit brain
An send a hunner sun-blinn't wave-tipp't gulls
Tae skriegh thur fremit wurds for me back hame.

# Slugs

*George T. Watt*

Div slugs ken thay ar universally reviled?
div thair mithers warn thaim,
kep awa frae the beer
an that it's nae trui fit thay sey aboot saut
it disnae hairden yer arteries.
Or ar thay left tae fen fur thairsels
me an yer paw, we'r fur the guidlife.

Fan A mow the girse
fitwey hae worms nae learnt
kep yer heids doun?
Fur years A'd toss thaim aside
juist tae save thaim frae the blade
but thay nivver developed wings
evolution's nae aa it's cracked up tae be
mibbie Darwin haesnae thocht it oot richt.

A ponner thay things as a chyave awaa
*Ein Heldenleben's* nae me,
A'm fur the fit sudjer, heid doun
rakin up the girse cuttins fur the slaw decline,
but the spuggies chirp awaa in the buss,
the daffies glint thair ee as A pass
thankfu fur the wee tait seaweed
that kep the slugs at bay.

# Virgil's Last Flight

*Mike Russell*

When the vet came out of the living room looking solemn Rosie Renwick realised that her biodrive was going to die. Knowing that she knew that he knew that she knew the truth, the vet just stood there, rubbing his beard, his eyes on the floor. There were no words required. But as well as sensitive he was also trained to be positive. The Astaroth worm had torn through Rosie's model of biodrive; though the vet's bedside manner was polished he wasn't meek and respectful for very long, not when there was upselling to be done.

'The new model of aviform biodrive does not have the same vulnerabilities,' he informed her. 'Your insurance, I believe, will cover a replacement.'

The vet was being practical, but Rosie wasn't that comfortable with the idea of getting a new biodrive just as quickly as if it were a pair of socks. Virgil had been with her for seven years. Virgil wasn't just rewritable organic memristors.

'That sounds pretty final to me,' she said, not meaning to sound quite so snappy.

'I've done everything I can,' said the vet, taken aback. Behind dark-framed optics his dark eyes widened. Customers didn't usually bark at him like this. 'The protein registries, the gene cores,' he protested, 'they're all being purged on a pico-second cycle. But the malware code keeps hiding. All the cores are fatally compromised and they won't support digital storage. I'm sorry, Ms Renwick, your aviform biodrive will have to be replaced.'

'His name is Virgil,' said Rosie, her temper rising again.

The vet softened his tone.

'OK. Virgil. You've had him a long time – I know how it is. I would feel the same way.'

From the pocket of the vet's work-jacket that hung behind the kitchen door, a small white rat with pink eyes poked its head out. Its selected voice was gruff and casual.

'Stop – I'm welling up here. You got four new messages. Martin wants you at the Grainger place, like an hour ago. Three kids, five grandchildren – that's a lot of technology under one fancy roof, and a lot of ignorance. Seven per cent of last year's turnover is getting impatient.'

The vet glanced at Rosie.

'If I could just make this call...'

She ignored him. 'I want to see Virgil, before you... you dispose of him, or whatever it is you do.'

The vet nodded. 'Sure,' he said, his calm professionalism restored. 'That's not a problem.' To his biodrive, he said: 'Gimme base, Coco.'

Coco's tiny pink eyes flashed, pelt rippling from green to red and back again to white as his DNA bits flipped at exaflop speed. He placed the call.

'To hear is to obey.'

The vet strode into the hallway, his finger to his ear-bud. 'Hi Martin, if you can tell Mrs Grainger we'll have someone there within half an hour.' The door closed on the rest of the conversation. 'No, I think you should tell her...'

Evidently, Coco was unaffected by the Astaroth worm. Rosie didn't suppose it would do the vet's reputation any good if his own biodrive had succumbed. The thing would be firewalled to the max. Rats – ugh! How male a predilection. She eyed Coco with distaste, and he wisely sank back into the vet's jacket pocket without another word. She washed out two handcrafted coffee cups and hung them on stainless steel hooks, conscious of the meeting she had to attend in little over an hour.

Oh well, Rosie thought, at least most of her files were safe, including all the important ones. She'd lost a few of her older photos and documents, but she hadn't looked at either for a long time. Everything she needed or wanted had been cloud-banked milli-seconds after the worm had started on Virgil's gene cores, tripping the safety flush.

She hadn't spoken about Virgil in those terms for a long time. He wasn't just two pounds of chromo-gel and graphene neuronics. He was wisdom and intelligence, alive to the oceans of wideband that washed over the world. Sometimes, Rosie wondered if Virgil wasn't keeping her as a pet. Perhaps their relationship was... unbalanced.

She no longer felt embarrassed when she thought of him as a friend. She cleared her throat. 'Excuse me, Coco, isn't it?'

She saw movement in the jacket pocket and a moment later a pointed white snout poked out.

'I'm sorry for the delay, Ms Renwick,' Coco began with practised insincerity. 'I'm sure Kenny... our, ah, agent, will be...'

'It isn't that,' she cut in. 'I'm just wondering if I can go in to see Virgil – now. If he does have to be... offlined, or whatever, I'd like to say goodbye.'

The rat's pelt flashed, primary coloured computation dappling its surface.

'I guess,' said Coco. 'So long as you don't touch any of our stuff.'

Rosie glared at the rat until it disappeared back into the vet's pocket.

In the living room, Virgil the woodpecker biodrive sat in the centre of a glass-topped coffee table, hunkering down, wings folded, surrounded by wires and mini-screens and a belt-roll of slender, precision tools. His plumage had turned dark blue, almost black in places. It was hard to tell if his eyes were open or not, and every now and then a weak pulse of colour brightened on his feathers, feeble glimpses of light. Near him, the largest diagnostic screen silently scrolled columns of assembly language.

Virgil's sharp beak twitched.

'I hate being this boring colour, it's depressing. But I guess that's the least of my worries.'

Rosie looked pensive, troubled, then remembered the good news she had to tell him.

'I heard earlier that they're close to catching the black hats. They think the worm comes from somewhere in South Korea. They'll be able to brain-scan the perps and encipher a cure.'

'Hmm,' said Virgil, resettling his wings. 'Maybe. But it'll come too late for me.'

'You don't know that.'

'I do. Kenny told me.'

'What – just like that?'

'I asked him. So he told me straight.' Virgil shook his head, moaning. 'I feel like I've been turned inside out and dipped in acid.'

'I'm sorry.'

'It's not your fault.'

'I must have opened something I shouldn't, an attachment.'

'No, this is a worm – they spread by themselves, with no user action.' Virgil adjusted his position, tucking his head further into his plumage. 'It's a common misconception.'

They were quiet for a moment, Virgil with his eyes closed. Was he asleep, or dead?

'Have a look at this,' he said, suddenly rousing himself.

Two splaying beams of light shot from Virgil's eyes and formed flickering video footage at a perfect height for Rosie to observe. The image kept twitching and defocusing, coarse-grained around the edges, as the worm attacked the chromosomal storage of digital information. A sigil, ancient seal of Astaroth, tried to superimpose itself over the footage, blinking subliminally as the biodrive's gene cores were continually purged by Kenny's kit. System integrity was on life-support.

Gasping with delight, Rosie put her hands to her face.

'Northumberland. Jane and Peter, and Jane's mum. We're walking to Craster, this little fishing village along the coast.' She laughed. 'I'd forgotten you'd taken this.'

Virgil wasn't surprised.

'You'd bought me three weeks before. Hardly knew what I could do, then.'

The file played. Small spots of white and yellow glinted on Virgil's dark feathers, and disappeared, as he showed her the holiday footage. Higher function activity was hard to maintain in his weakened state.

Walkers on a narrow sandy track. A beautiful day. Backpacks and boots and a bird's eye view of it all. Snippets of chat as Virgil flew in low and swept past the group; Jane's mum saying something about the standard of food on a Nile cruise. Her son-in-law laughing; Virgil arcing into the blue sky and the sound of talking faded.

He perched on the walls of a ruined castle, zooming in on a sunburnt Rosie and the others picking their way along the path, some 200 yards below. Then the group was in a busy pub, munching on fish and chips, trying the local beer. Virgil looked down on them, from the top of an old upright piano if Rosie remembered correctly. All the tables were occupied by at least one person. There were a few other biodrives in the pub, dogs and birds mainly.

Rosie watched the excerpt of a holiday she'd taken with friends nearly seven years before. Jane's mother was dead and Peter had been sacked in the interim. Time had gone by and, sad to say, Virgil might well have started off as a 30th birthday present to herself, but she wondered who knew her better, now. Did anyone even come close? He automatically deleted crap photos; he rescheduled appointments, ordered provisions, did most of the groundwork for presentations, and always seemed to say the right thing when she needed to hear it. Virgil was the only dependable sentient being in her life. And he would no longer be perched on the fridge when she was eating; on the bedpost when he woke her with an early alarm call; pushing her on if she tried to skip a gym session.

She'd have to accept the fact the he was as good as gone. There were practicalities to consider.

'I'm afraid this is too corrupted to risk transferring to your new biodrive,' said Virgil, eyes ablaze with the playbeams. 'It's a shame, for you.'

'And for you,' said Rosie, quiet at the sight of her younger self.

Virgil grunted, unmoved. He closed the file that would die with him, his eyes becoming dark. The air emptied of holiday fun. There was silence in Rosie's embedded ear-mikes.

She was glad to turn away. She tapped on the wall and a screen appeared; a flood of new emails. It had been 72 hours since her emergency cloud-bank had been tripped, and Virgil had not taken a single incoming message or file in that time. He was getting bored with being useless. If he couldn't be of use it was time to call time. What he had learned, everything he'd processed and experienced in seven years, would become part of the master program. It would not be lost. The metadata would be used to improve the next generation of biodrive. He would have played his part in aviform evolution.

'Unplug me from all this shit and open the window, will you?'

Rosie turned from her email, open-mouthed.

'Please,' said Virgil.

'But – why?'

'So I can fly around the garden.'

'You don't have the energy, the co-ordination.'

'I can get both – if you tell the vet to do what I say.'

Rosie's eyes narrowed.

'And what might that be?'

There was a pause.

'Reroute cellular photovoltaics to motor control; introduce a bottom-up terminator protocol for gene registry logic-gate switching.'

She looked blank.

'I stop being an intelligent machine and end up as just a bird,' Virgil explained. 'Then I'll run out of power and die. It'll take about two mintues, all in. But it'll be the best two minutes I'm ever going to have.' He gave an awkward little shrug. 'Please.'

Rosie slid open the patio doors and a bright green and yellow woodpecker shot out. No longer was the flashing of recombinase computation muted, the plumage dark; Virgil glittered and shone as he arrowed into the sky and over the high hedge that ran along the bottom of the garden.

'It's all about how you go,' he shouted as he flew. 'Not sitting round waiting for the end, playing it safe. If your time is short then use it. People waste too much of it because they don't realise how...'

He curved away over the neighbouring rooftops, and Rosie couldn't hear what he said after that. She waited. The vet appeared at her shoulder, and they both watched from the stone veranda.

The garden was quiet. The grass glistened from an earlier rain-shower.

They saw Virgil return, sagging with every downbeat. He circled the garden, swooping down, wings angled to pull out of the dive. Up again he rose, with effort, then lost control of his wings and veered wildly into the trunk of a thick beech. With a single squawk he crashed to the ground, a dark feathery hump at the bottom of the garden. Turing-testable intelligence had been transformed into hazardous waste. Virgil would be disposed of, in accordance with regulations, in an out-of-town incinerator.

For a few seconds Rosie stood at the window, shocked by what she'd seen. Virgil was gone.

But then she remembered the time, thought of the full working week that lay ahead, and where she had to be in exactly 41 minutes.

'Oh dear,' said the vet, tutting to himself. 'I'd better go and get it.'

At the bottom of the garden he knelt, his back to the house. He opened a small chromium case and took out a bladed tool. Careful not to be seen, he made a few incisions along Virgil's spine and neck and pulled the graphene head and column free from the boneless organics. Since the Astaroth worm had run riot, some customers had expressed an interest in keeping the head, as a momento mori, but it was better not to let them see how it was removed from their dead biodrive. Kenny unscrewed the neuronic column, wiped chunks of chromo-gel away, and sprayed the feathered head with sterilsing fluid. He gave it a wipe-over, placed the spinal column and organics in his case and snapped it shut.

Rosie agreed: keeping Virgil's head was a great idea. She'd put it on the mantlepiece in the living room, between her Kenyan carvings.

'You will of course need a new biodrive,' said Kenny, sounding as respectful as he could.

Placing the dark head in her chosen spot, Rosie stepped back to see how it looked. Virgil would be forever vigilant, his jet black eyes fixed on the room. He'd have liked that. He would never be forgotten.

'Yes,' she said. 'I suppose I will.'

Kenny worked the opening, rubbing his beard as if mulling a thought.

'Tell you what, I've got the latest aviform model, a kestrel, in the van. I can get you going on one within 10 minutes if you like?'

He also had reconditioned Virgils for under five grand, but he'd hold those as a fallback.

Rosie considered the offer.

'You don't have any barn owls, do you?'

# Freud is Dead

*Ever Dundas*

'My eyes have been giving me so much trouble, but since I was thrown out of the eye pavilion I've been going to Black and Lizars. They're very good.'

Ann tapped her fingers against the table as she spoke, and Jane nodded. They sat in silence for a moment. Ann patted at her coiffed grey hair. It was held so perfectly in place that it didn't move at her touch.

'Is my hair OK?'

'It's fine,' said Jane.

'Just fine? Oh, God. That breeze was terrible. I knew it would wreak havoc.'

'It's perfect, stop fussing.'

'I'm not fussing, you said it was fine. Then you said it was perfect. Either it's fine or it's perfect, which is it?'

'You set it back in place, so *now* it's perfect.'

Ann smiled smugly, and settled into her chair with a satisfied jiggle. She let out a contented sigh.

'Pass that chair over.'

'What?' said Jane.

'The chair, that chair. Next to you.'

Jane stood and pushed the chair over to Ann.

'You'll have to excuse me, Jane. I really must prop my leg up. It's been giving me such trouble lately.'

Ann propped her leg up on the chair, her trouser leg bunching up a little as she got her leg into a comfortable position. Ann let out a harrumphing noise that signalled to Jane she was about to start on about her leg. Jane dug into her cake as distraction, but paused mid-stab and gawped at Ann's leg.

'Are those tights you're wearing? Under your trousers. Are those tights?'

'No, of course not! Look,' Ann said as she pulled the trouser leg up further, 'they stop just above the ankle. I never wear tights. These are socks. Look, you can see.'

'But they look like tights.'

Ann held up her trouser leg and scowled at Jane.

'They're socks that look like tights, but they're not tights. I would never wear tights.'

Ann pulled at the top of the sock for emphasis. Jane frowned at Ann's leg, her fork hovering above her forgotten cake. A small man sidled up to them, the top of his head just reaching the tabletop. His face was wide, tanned, and expressionless, his eyes an almost translucent grey. His crumpled suit swamped him. Ann and Jane were so busy contemplating Ann's puzzling socks-not-tights that they didn't notice him.

'But they look *so* like tights.'

'Yes, but they only go a little past the ankle. They're made to look like tights, but really they're socks.'

The man reached up and took Jane's cake, clasping it in his hand, the icing oozing through his fingers.

'Tights-socks.'

'No, not tights. Socks that look like tights. They're socks. I would never wear tights.'

The man crouched down and shuffled underneath their table. He crossed his legs and began eating the cake.

Ann haughtily pulled her trouser-leg back over her ankle.

'OK,' said Jane, 'but they look like tights.'

Jane released the hovering fork, only to find crumbs and smeared icing. She stared at her plate.

'They're supposed to look like tights,' said Ann. 'But I would *never* wear tights.'

Jane jabbed at the plate with her fork, as if the cake was invisible and she simply had to locate it.

'Pig,' Ann mumbled, 'She distracted me with my socks and ate all that to herself. Didn't even offer a single bite. Pig.'

'What was that?' said Jane, still staring at her empty plate. 'I can't quite hear as I used to.'

'Well, if you stopped clattering around with that plate, you could hear me perfectly.'

Jane laid down the fork.

'So, what did you say?'

'I *said*, what did you do yesterday?'

'Oh, yesterday! Yes, yesterday. Well, not much. Handwashing sweaters all day.'

'You handwash your sweaters?'

'Yes. Of course. Don't you?'

'Oh no. I put them in the machine.'

'But you can't wash them in the machine, they're so delicate.'

'Washing sweaters in the machine is fine. A nice gentle wash and they're fine.'

'A gentle wash?'

'Yes, and they're fine. Complete waste of the day, handwashing.'

'Ah, I suppose it was.'

Ann's smug smile settled back into her face.

'A nice gentle wash in future and you'll be free to do whatever you please.'

Two twentysomething girls clattered their way to the table next to Jane and Ann. Their spindly limbs and huge black sunglasses gave them an insect-like appearance.

'You know, she's so beautiful she intimidates me,' said Lucy, an unlit cigarette dangling from her fingers. 'I get all tongue-tied kinda and say the most stupid things. I know it's silly, but do you know what I mean getting intimidated by beautiful people?'

They sat at slight angles from each other, facing away, languidly draped over their chairs.

'Yeah, I think I know that kind of feeling you're talking about,' replied Justyna, speaking slowly. 'I'm intimidated when I meet with you.'

'You're intimidated by me?'

'Yeah. I become nervous and don't know what to say.'

'But you always have lots to say. You don't seem nervous.'

'I say lots to hide my nerves.'

'Why would I intimidate you? I really don't understand.'

'You're so mysterious and strange.'

'I'm mysterious? You're crazy. Almost as crazy as the French.'

They laugh. Lucy sips on her coffee, and Justyna eats her cake, staring out across the café with blank insect eyes.

'I still have to handwash the silks,' said Jane.

'Whatever for?'

'They're so delicate. Silk.'

'You can wash silk in the machine. A very nice gentle wash does the job.'

'Yes, I suppose it does.'

'Really if you can't deal with your silks and your sweaters you should have a maid in, once a week at least.'

'A maid?'

'Yes, once a week, but not anymore than that or they start to take liberties.'

'Liberties?'

'Yes, liberties. But they're quite cheap, if you get them from Mexico, or Poland. Mind you, Jane, they're letting in too many foreigners these days. We're a small island, and we're practically overrun. We have all these homegrown doctors and nurses looking for work but all the foreigners have their jobs and they just start taking liberties thinking they can do what they like. Everyone really must abide by the rules of the country they're in, but we're just going crazy with their human rights.'

'Oh, yes,' said Jane, 'it's appalling.'

Jane's eyes glazed over, and she glanced over towards Justyna and Lucy.

'By the way, I'm not a lesbian,' said Justyna.

Jane perked up and leaned over, straining to hear Justyna and Lucy as Ann droned on.

'You're not?' said Lucy. 'I didn't think you were.'

'If we go to Iran or Iraq,' continued Ann, 'we don't drink alcohol because we would be punished.'

Ann tapped her fingers on Jane's saucer to get her full attention.

'And they come here and do whatever they like and everyone goes on about human rights.'

As her tea rocked, rattling and spilling on to the table, Jane paid attention to Ann again. She steadied the cup and nodded.

'We welcome them and they pay us back by loathing and hating us. You know I'm not racist, I was never racist, but there's just too many of them. We don't see many here but when I was in London they were everywhere, plenty of them working in cafés and things and very sullen. I was very tolerant.'

'Oh, yes, I know you are. Very tolerant.'

Jane slid her tea to the end of the table, out of Ann's reach. She shuffled her chair back, inch by inch, her head tilted towards Lucy and Justyna.

'My boyfriend was worried by our correspondence.'

'Oh?'

'I read out to him what we were saying and he said we sounded like two lesbians. He thought we were going to get together to kiss. He wanted to know when I'd be home.'

Jane leaned further towards the girls.

'I've always been tolerant,' said Ann. 'I have friends who go to Pakistan.'

'Well,' said Lucy, 'you can appreciate another woman's beauty without being a lesbian.'

'I suppose.'

'But I'm in-between.'

'In-between?'

'Yeah, I'm not a lesbian, but I'm not straight. I'm in-between.'

'Are you sure?'

'Pretty sure.' 'Weird.'

'...and so I do think if the bankers do their job, they should be rewarded.'

Ann stopped and stared at Jane, realising she had been listening to the girls and not her.

'Jane? Are you listening?'

'Yes, Ann...'

'If a banker brings in 5k then I don't see anything wrong with awarding him 2k. We *should* be awarding him. It's good for our economy.'

'"Him"? Who's "him"?'

'The banker.'

'What banker?'

'Any banker. They should be rewarded for helping the economy.'

'Didn't they hurt the economy?'

'Oh, don't listen to the socialists dear. They'd have us handwashing sweaters every day if they could.'

Ann stopped talking and sipped on her tea, overhearing Lucy and Justyna's conversation.

'I've never understood the gay or straight thing,' said Lucy, as Ann choked on her tea and Jane giggled. 'If you fall in love, you fall in love. I don't see what it matters whether they have a cunt or a cock or both or neither.'

'Oh,' said Justyna.

'Oh!' said Ann.

The small man stood at Justyna and Lucy's table, but they didn't notice him.

'I'm sure Freud would say that was abnormal.'

'Freud can suck my cock.'

'You don't have a cock.'

'How do you know?'

The small man took a cigarette from Lucy's packet.

'There you are, being mysterious again.'

'Anyway, Freud is dead.'

'I guess.'

The girls sat silently drinking their coffee as Ann and Jane gathered their things.

'Never in my life!' said Ann, eyeing Lucy and Justyna as Jane tried to suppress her laughter by shoving her scarf in her mouth.

'Jane, whatever are you doing? It's not as if you haven't had enough to eat with all that cake.'

Jane spat out the scarf, making a small choking sound and continued listening to the girls as Ann fumbled with her coat.

'My first kiss was a girl,' said Lucy.

'Mine too.'

'I thought you weren't a lesbian.'

'I'm not. It was at school.'

'Oh.'

'We had an orgy in a forest.'

'An orgy?'

'Yeah.'

'But you're Catholic.'

'I was young.'

'I guess.'

Lucy and Justyna were silent for a moment and the man under their table smoked the stolen cigarette.

'Lucy?'

'Mmm?'

'Our table is on fire.'

Ann dragged a giggling Jane by the hand and purposefully knocked the girls' table, giving a snort of disapproval.

'See what happens when immigrants and dwarves are let in the country, Jane – moral decrepitude.'

Lucy and Justyna slipped under the table and sat with the man, sharing the cigarette.

'I never thought of sitting *under* the table,' said Lucy.

'Me either,' said Justyna.

'It's a whole new perspective.'

'You can study people's feet.'

'That woman,' the man said, gesturing to the disappearing figure of Ann, 'She was wearing tights under her trousers.'

'Weird,' said Justyna.

'Weird,' said Lucy.

# Starbucks

*Tendai Huchu*

The low status male sits at the table next to the glass front in Starbucks, George St. He stares at the pricelist, a selection of hot and cold beverages, each costing, roughly, thirty minutes' wages. A wave of righteous indignation washes over him; he is outraged at the scam, the broad daylight, shameless, barefaced robbery of it all. To imagine that the five minutes it takes to sip his mix of (in no particular order) sugar, ground coffee beans, hot water – served in a cheap, logoed, glazed ceramic mug – is the pecuniary equivalent of him breaking his back over a half hour period, cleaning up after consumers at the retail unit he works in, strikes him as manifestly unjust. In this analysis of the situation, he neglects to factor that Mr/Mrs/Ms Starbucks is not just providing him with the drink; i.e. the cost of his beverage must also factor, rates, rent, advertising, inventory, damaged merchandise, utilities, insurance, taxes (if not, then payments to tax avoidance specialists), salaries/wages/commissions, shareholders' interests, etcetera, etcetera.

After sitting in the café for fifteen minutes, not yet having purchased anything, the lsm begins to feel a sense of shame and every time the barista looks at him it feels as though she is able to see though his clothing to his wallet which contains:

1) Bus pass
2) Tesco Clubcard
3) Nectar card
4) Expired gym membership card
5) Driver's licence
6) Coinage in the following denominations: 1x£1, 1x£0.50, 4x£0.10, 1x£0.05, 7x£0.01
7) Nationwide debit card: balance of -£105.22
8) Lint

She (the female acquaintance he is waiting for) is late. She said she would be there at four o'clock. It is now quarter past four. This whole thing was her idea. He was just minding his own business, trying to keep his nose above the waterline, when she called and said that she wanted to "talk." The lsm has read enough popular psychology to know that her lateness is an ominous indication of what's to come. So, not only does he have to endure the shame inducing attentions of the barista, he also has to deal with the fact that, in all likelihood, he is about to get dumped.

In this moment, he feels like he is walking the plank, blindfolded, hands tied behind his back, the pointy end of a cutlass embedded somewhere in his lumbar region between L3 and L5. He needs only wait for the cool embrace of the ocean, in which fins are circling, to complete the picture.

"Talk" is all she ever seems to want to do. He doesn't have the energy for it. Just last week, he read about something called decision fatigue. He's sure that's what he suffers from, along with several other undiagnosed mental health conditions of varying severity. He looks out the window to the road where cars drive up and down. Caucasian women with shopping bags walk alongside blank-faced Caucasian males, a runner in lycra jogs (why in the middle of the city centre?), and no sign of his beloved.

He's already had to shrug off the attentions of some random dude who wanted to talk to him about the weather. Nice sunny day, isn't it? Rhetorical? Duh, I'm not blind, I can see the sun, just like you, I can feel the heat. Hope it holds out, it might rain you know. Who the fuck are you, the weatherman?

For a moment, he thinks about exercising his constitutional rights, getting up and leaving. But if he leaves before "the talk" then there will be a "talk about 'the talk'", and that very prospect fills him with despair. Fortunately/unfortunately she arrives. Somehow he did not see her come in.

He gets up, kisses her on the left cheek, goes for the right but she has already sat down. Generally, the lsm is wary of PDAs, but the situation being what it is, he, at least, must be seen to try.

– Sorry I'm late.

– That's alright. I only just got here myself.

– The traffic was awful.

– You look great. God, how I've missed you. I was going to call when I got your text.

She favours him with a polite smile. It pleases him that she is wearing the thirty man-hour necklace he bought her from Argos for her birthday. It's white gold, and the pendant hangs over her collar bone, accentuating the slenderness of her neck. He feels like biting it.

– Would you like some coffee?

Secretly, he wishes that she would offer to pay for it since this entire excursion is her idea, but he should be so lucky.

– A chai crème Frappuccino please, she says, and as he is about to go she adds: Oh, can you get me a chocolate brownie swirl? I'm starving, it's been hectic today.

Great, now he's going to spend an hour and a half's wages for this. Why do we even have to "talk" in Starbucks, he wonders. There are many different ways of talking, both ancient and modern, that simply don't involve him adding to his -£105.22 overdraft.

The barista smiles as she sucks the juice out of his debit card.

– Enjoy your drinks, she says – as if that's possible.

The lsm goes to the pick-up counter and waits with a group of university type douchebags discussing an exhibition at the National Gallery. He is forced to listen to their arty, farty talk about flat tones, negative spaces, swirlings, flowings, subtleties... and it becomes immediately clear, to him at least, that their conversation is nothing but crass regurgitation of bullshit from a brochure. He is relieved when he is called up to receive his order, including his Americano.

– Do you know the difference between an Americano and regular filter coffee? he asks one of the douches.

– Huh? Is that a trick question?

– It's all in the preparation, he says and leaves them to ponder it over.

He arrives at the table wearing a slight smirk, the self-satisfaction of having got one over on the petite bourgeoisie. This quickly dampens down when she asks him to bring her a fork and serviette. It's the word "serviette" that gets to him – servant, service, servile, servitude – the latent classist connotations Marx would have seen through. Marx would have said: Get your own bloody serviette.

The lsm's awareness of his lower class status makes him overly sensitive to any gesture, word, or act that might in fact be evidence of microaggression from better-off members of society. His blood is full of cortisol and free radicals. Only thirty, tiny crows-feet (or the beginnings of) show at the sides of his eyes.

– I've been thinking about us and the future, she says.

– Uh huh, he replies, projecting himself somewhere in the twenty fifth century – starships and phasers. He can barely maintain his grasp on the present, let alone dwell on some imagined future, but he dares not air this view.

– We really need to figure out where we're going.

She takes a bite out of the chocolate brownie swirl which he calculates to be worth anywhere between ten and fifteen minutes of hard labour. Then he takes a sip of his coffee and waits for her to continue.

– I'm a band 5 staff nurse...

Another microaggression – a reminder of social status. He is firmly Seg Grade D according to the NRS classification from the last poll he took. That's working class, semi and unskilled manual workers, one short rung above the dole and state pensioners. She is two rungs above, C1.

– ... and I think that we have to start thinking about your future. At your age you can't be renting a room like you're a twenty year old student...

Another microaggression – a reminder of his age in relation to his domiciliary circumstances. He allows this one to pass without even thinking about it, mondo Zen, like he's Nelson Mandela. She's grown up; you can hear it from the way she speaks. She sounds like her mum; she's five years younger than him, but she's already paying into a pension plan! The lsm is constantly worrying about whether she really loves him or not; how and why would a babe like her fall for a gororo like him?

– ... you need to do something to uplift yourself. Go to college, do a course. For Christ's sake, you dropped out of medical school. I mean, who does that...

In his defence, that was years ago, and he didn't want to go to uni in the first place but his loser dad forced him into it. Yes, he could think about it, how he could have spent his life strutting about with a stethoscope around his neck, checking out hot nurses in A&E,

a BMW in the driveway and MRSA in his skin flora. Instead, the lsm engages in nihilistic practices prevalent in, but not exclusive to, his socioeconomic grouping, including, but not limited to, the excessive consumption of alcohol, tobacco, stimulants and depressants; ingesting anything that alters his state of consciousness to give himself reprieve from the soul-destroying pain of his quotidian reality. But whichever way you spin it, dropping out of uni was a dumb move (economically) and a contributory factor to his downward social mobility.

– ... it's time to stop wallowing in self-pity and take charge of your life...

To try and remedy the situation, he has taken to spending at least an hour's wages each week on scratch cards and the lucky dip for the Lotto. He has also staked his future on horses, greyhounds and football in the hope of one day hitting the jackpot. The lsm's life is entirely at the mercy of global stock markets and government policy, none of which he has any control or influence over. How can he even begin to explain the situation to her, to make her aware of *his* reality.

– ... Are you even listening to me?

– Yes. Of course I am.

– What did I just say? She sounds just like the voice on the tannoy, the one that instructs him to go mop up spilt milk in aisle 7 or cooking oil in aisle 23.

– I could do with a smoke. Can we go outside?

She rolls her eyes, then looks at him, the incredulity seeping out cruelly and slapping him in the face. He shrugs, then wears a what-the-fuck-did-I-do-this-time? face.

– I don't have to stick around for this bullshit, if you didn't want to "talk", why didn't you just say so, she says and makes to rise from the chair.

– Okay, please, I'm sorry. I get absent minded like that. You know me, babes, my mind just drifts sometimes. But I'm here. I want to "talk."

– Pay attention. It's really important for us to "talk" about this.

– Yes, ma'am.

– Look, be sarcastic if you want, but the future is important. You're not getting any younger, y'know. We should move in together, take the next step. I want to know what you think...

He looks at her lips moving. Her philtrum is the cutest part of her, the way it forms a perfect convex groove, an 11. He is sure the middle aged woman reading Amos Tutuola at the next table is listening to their conversation. The stuff his girlfriend is saying comes at him in a concussive blast wave, the kinetic energy shattering every molecule in his cranium. She is stunningly beautiful. A half-twisted smile forms on his face.

– ... oh God, I can't take this anymore. What is wrong with you?!

She bursts into tears. A torrent, a river flows down her face and she buries her face in her hands and with it the frustration of trying to communicate with a dumb object. The lsm opens his mouth, moves his jaw up and down, expelling air, but he knows whatever he says will be inadequate.

# Things I Have Found in the Junction Street Post Box

*Lynsey May*

175,563 letters, assorted. Envelopes typed and handwritten, backs licked or stuck with Sellotape, Gaffa Tape and, once, a plaster. The blue kind you're given if you work in catering. The same ones Marie would leave balled up by the edge of the sink, slippery on the counter and reminding me to give her a kiss and ask about her day.

100,785 cards. Recognisable by their stiffness, the stupid cartoons on the envelopes, novelty stamps and careful handwriting (except for in the run up to Christmas, when the addresses get sloppy). You can tell when they have something extra inside by the thickness, but you'll never find pound coins in them anymore.

56 gloves, eight being pairs and most black and woolly. Overall, there've been more women's gloves than men's, and there was one black leather pair that sparked off a particular fantasy and I passed many long hours of my morning shift imagining them on Marie's hands, adding a little something to our bedtime routine.

117 flattened beer cans, 34 soft drinks cans in a similar condition. Normally empty, but small spatters of their insides sometimes patterned the envelopes. Kind of thing the boy will be doing soon, no doubt. The smell of beer cans that've been sitting in a post box all night is enough to make your stomach churn, especially when you've been up late hitting the bottle yourself.

One engagement ring. I asked in Lost and Found about that more than once, but no one ever came to pick it up. Told Marie about it at the time. Said wasn't it awful, the thought of that poor girl, frantic, not knowing what happened to her ring? Marie said it was probably a fake, costume jewellery or something.

19 mobile phones, from brand new to completely banjoed. There's been a few I've considered keeping for myself, well, for the boy really – he's always banging on about wanting one of those smartphones – but I handed them all in. Phones like them, they're the kind of thing someone comes looking for and the last thing I'm needing is more trouble. The boy probably only would have ended up breaking it anyway.

10 slices of pizza. Typically, these will have something especially disgusting on top, like anchovies or kebab meat, but more than once I've fished out a pepperoni or margarita. I have never been tempted to eat one.

1002 postcards. I always read the back, even though the messages are normally all the same and really quite depressing. There was once a series of saucy ones, and I enjoyed handing them over to the sorting office, knowing I'd be passing a smile on to someone there.

But after the first five or six I started getting a weird feeling about them, thinking it might be someone sending them to themselves – something about the details, the perfect handwriting, the way nothing new ever seemed to really change – and I stopped enjoying them after that.

Approximately 2783 crisp and sweet wrappers. I lost count one day, and haven't been right on the button since. Six times, the chocolate bars have still been in their wrappers, only a little bashed up. Seeing them reminds me of the boy, who, when he was young, used to pick any old sweet up off the ground and shove it straight in his gob, covered in fluff and hair and dirt. You had to hook a finger behind his small, sharp teeth to drag whatever shite it was out.

27 purses and 26 wallets. Most had bank cards with a name on them, some had a few pictures, which I looked at and tended to think about for a couple of days afterwards, although I never went to ask at Lost and Found whether any of them had been collected or not. I don't like to say it, but I have taken a little money from these now and then. Only recently mind, only when I've found myself short, and not enough that anyone would really notice. Or care.

Eight condoms. Three still in their wrappers, presumably jettisoned in frustration. One blown up like a skinny balloon, bouncing around in the box. Four used, picked up between two envelopes and dumped into the bin by the Bookies, as I tried not to think about who used them or how.

12 sets of keys. A hangover from the days when lost sets of keys could be posted and returned by the identifying address on their chains – not that any of the keys I found ever had a return address. When Marie changed the locks, I almost did the same with my own, was going to slot them into the box at Elm Row. But they're still in my pocket.

98 needles. Sometimes used but with the cap thoughtfully replaced, but more often bare and waiting to stick you. We're meant to wear special gloves, but I normally just turn the yellow pouch inside out, put my hand in, and operate it like a glove puppet. Then I fold it back the right way out, covering up the needle ready for safe disposal.

Seven envelopes with no name or address on the front. I opened all of these. Two were thank you notes, one a cancellation for a magazine subscription and three were only cheques for bills.

One was a love letter from a young woman, maybe a teenager, who wrote things that were very hopeful. That one stayed in my locker for a while, but once the bastarding lawyer told me I'd never get even weekend custody without a place of my own, it joined me in my new flat. It's nice to look at and have a bit of a think, because that girl, she doesn't know what happened to her letter now does she? And anyway, she's only a young thing, with plenty more letters to write.

# The House Where I Was Born

*Diana Hendry*

The ghosts are easy. I can switch them on
like a tv soap. Here's Pa going up the stairs,
flattened back of his slippers going slip slap
and Ma in the kitchen, her cigarette ash stretching
precariously over the black frying pan. One sister
in her room of make-up, petticoats, sequins,
the other sobbing over her boarding school trunk
and my various selves flitting about age this
that, the other. Here I am – flash – and here –
and here. Do I really have to say the Lord's Prayer
twenty times without making a mistake? Am I
still at it? Voices in the garden. The cough
on the stairs. The wooden gate. Spots of time.
The house that mothered me more than mother.

Somehow the memory of it's gone shabby
as if it needs fresh paint, the windows cleaned.
A silent, sullen child stares out, closes the door.

# Maiden

*Dorothy Alexander*

I was a **maiden** and I wanted to play.

I wanted to be a little bird, an Icarus
girl, whose **feather**s cut the horizon
and do not slither. But I feared colour
as I feared flame; white **on** white
brought me joy. The secrets of my
heart's **razor**ed strata were obscured
by sleight of mouth so that the
damage hung from **wire** attached to
trick skin,

and meaning became a
**shadow**, a smudge of **red**.

# The Tent

*J Johannesson Gaitán*

It squeals mighty hell when you try to make it a home. Likes to keep its pimples fresh and
bitter like the pride of coffee at fifteen. If you don't add sugar. If you hold on to the rims
and tell them that you like it too.

    It takes only a parking space.

The tent says it's glad to see you again, but the wind makes it sound like *be* you: swallow
you, with wellies and all three hours out of a city's reach. The cold is like your dad: a
mathematician. Worrying still for your miscalculations.

    And when it laughs it sounds like snow.

Small people keep each other awake with their shivering. Over-sizing memory makes no
difference, to the rattle-snake of knee-caps next to fishing gear. We were here with a purpose
this time, to look for the bestseller in the bog. The tent says we like each other
        well enough.

# She woke atween Borrheid and Central

*Ross McGregor*

When the carriage moved oan fae Borrheid
she wakened, waitin
wance liftin her fair
tae let it faw again
wi clean and uncluttert
fawin

Even in the shakin
ae the long approach tae Glesga
she steyed still, then beginning
tae move her haunds
rubbin cream oan her face
wi firm circles puin
her een wider

Meenits fae Central she stertit her make-up
dabbin her heid wi foundation
layerin the paste
oan her cheeks
oan her chin
while others buttoned jaickets

She didnae rush herself
only a slight touch ae mascara
and a pooder blush
as the single track became twinty
the paintit wa's and paintit carriages passin
then stoappin tae jine aw the others
in the inside-oot licht ae the station

# If my gran had ever met Don Giovanni

*Jim Carruth*

If my gran had ever met Don Giovanni
she would've got the measure of the man
shown him her strong faith, stout resolve
gripping her bible as tight as a lover's hand

not succumbing to his sly and easy charm
as he whistled carefree by the byre door
setting himself as a lure in his own trap,
belly full of stolen fruits from her garden.

Her scowl was death sitting at your table
*You'll have had your tea then my lord.*
She'd utter just one line whose full stop
would be a barrel closing click at his back.

# An Erdlin cosmonaut's delyte on seein the Flag o Erd in anither galaxie

*Hamish Scott*

Hou gled tae see thir parsecs faur
the Flag o Erd, wir hamelt staur;
its green an blue the hert dis claur
nae maiter whaur

The green for aa Erd's growthe that hue;
for aa its waters rife the blue
an for the lift we traivelt throu
whan first we flew

# The First Language

*J Johannesson Gaitán*

Because one language was born two seconds behind the other, the other obstructed the
first one's world view. Things: become blurred and many-faced regardless of which eye you
use. They are not lies, says the Treasurer, but *face value*. You could choose to toss one back
– wish it safe landing.

    All fetal positions have moved on in their jet planes.

Because one pair of lungs hurried down the tear duct (its mother never smoked) this language
will get most girlfriends. Whether she wants them or not: she might want boyfriends. She
might want to live on an island outside the borders of land. They're both stunning making
faces under water:

    screaming obscenities behind the x-ray eye.

hub blubb
      burburbuja
        blublub
          jajahahajaja
            såpa

Nine months later a hand picks them up by the collar: time to sell. The Treasurer, is careful
not to damage the price of fur. One's legs are tied up with kisses, the other's with our local
sort of caress. Both are free to stumble down the highways, picking up experience as they
go. If they know
    how to distinguish them

from weeds, they might see each other again.

Because we require a birth order
    there's a divided song in the choir bench.

# Ferns

*Jane Bonnyman*

she cooked them with lime juice and butter
tiny spirals melted
slopped from the spoon like spinach
she breathed in their bitterness
at six she served them
with hard bread and onions
she knew from his face
and the way he pushed each one
to the side of the plate
that he was thinking of poison
those boys who died in the bush

he watched her stab them
with her fork lips glistening
she swallowed the lot
after dinner he heard her
lift the copper pan to its hook
pour some water from the jug
her steady steps on the stair

that night her stomach burned
red ants danced through her blood
she sweated into her clothes
listening to the tree frog cry like a child
and later a moth the size of a hummingbird
rested on her bed

she thought she saw fire in its eye
but in the drowsy coolness
it became a splinter of sunrise
caught in a giant unblinking lens.

# A Fine Talk

*Jane Bonnyman*

Let us find
that bright little café
opposite the harbour.
We can sit there
for twenty years
and watch each ship
come in, listening to
the rhythm of the sails
beating in the wind.

With a packet of tobacco
and a jug of wine
we can talk of art
and women
and the places
we found comfort in.

When we're deep
in conversation
the city will sink
the table, the chairs
the ships too -
then we'll go down.

Darkness comes,
the light from the café
shines like a firefly,
blinking intensely
for a time,
and without alarm,
is gone.

*The Gutter Interview:*
# Dilys Rose

Dilys Rose was born 1954 and brought up in Glasgow. She has won many awards for her work, including the Canongate Prize, the Macallan/Scotland on Sunday Short Story Competition and a Robert Louis Stevenson Memorial Award. Her poem 'Sailmaker's Palm' won the 2006 McCash Poetry Prize and her poetry collection Bodyworkwas shortlisted for the Sundial Scottish Arts Council Book Award. Rose's story collection *Red Tides* won the 1993 Scottish Arts Council Book Award and was shortlisted for both the Saltire Society Scottish Book of the Year Award and the McVitie's Prize for Scottish Writer of the Year.

Her published poetry includes *Madame Doubtfire's Dilemma*, (Chapman 1989), *When I Wear My Leopard Hat: Poems for Young Children*, illustrated by Gill Allan (Scottish Children's Press 1997), *Lure* (Chapman 2003), *Bodywork* (Luath 2007) and *Twinset* (2008), a T collaborative publication, with poet Karen Knight and illustrators Laurie Hastings and Polly Thelwell.

Dilys has published two novels, *Pest Maiden* (Headline Review 1999) and *Pelmanism* (Luath Press 2014) and several collections of short stories beginning with *Our Lady of the Pickpockets* (Secker & Warburg 1989), followed by *Red Tides* (Secker & Warburg 1993), *War Dolls* (Headline Review 1998) and *Lord of Illusions* (Luath Press 2005) and a collection of *Selected Stories* (Luath Press 2005).

She wrote the libretto for the chamber opera, *Kasper Hauser, Child of Europe* with the composer Rory Boyle and has collaborated with a number of other artists from different creative disciplines. Dilys is programme director of the Creative Writing Distance Learning programme at the University of Edinburgh.

**Gutter:** Where in Glasgow did you spend your childhood?

**DR:** The north-west. I spent the first seven or eight years living in the city and then my parents moved us out. I'm a bit reticent about my childhood, not for any particular reason other than it's not just my time, it's my parents' time as well. But I stayed in Glasgow, or around Glasgow, until I was seventeen. Then I left.

**Gutter:** And didn't come back?

**DR:** Well my parents subsequently moved so there was less reason to come back. I did work in Glasgow in the early 90s, I worked in Castlemilk as the first writer-in-residence and I really enjoyed coming back with a purpose.

**Gutter:** And were you involved in setting up *Cutting Teeth* [the literary magazine based in Castlemilk]?

**DR:** It was just beginning to be set up. They took the name that I wanted to use for something else [laughs]. It was happening around that time. By the time I left there was a magazine and there was also the small press, Wisdom Teeth, founded by

Graham Mackenzie.

**Gutter:** When did you leave home?

**DR:** I left Glasgow in 1971 to go to Edinburgh. Mainly, I wanted to go to a university and be away from home. Rather than go home for my tea at night, which so many students around Glasgow did.

**Gutter:** Where did that independence of mind come from? The whole tradition at that time in Glasgow was to stay at home.

**DR:** I don't know, it certainly didn't come from my parents. They didn't want me to leave, so I had to fight to leave and fight pretty hard. Maybe it was just a kind of stubbornness in me. Our family didn't do foreign holidays or anything at that time, and again I'd never been out of Britain till I was twenty, when I graduated and then I really wanted to get out and go travelling. I suppose I like things which are difficult. I did feel that I needed to get away. To do things my way as much as I could.

**Gutter:** Did it partly come from having had your horizons expanded through reading. Were you a reader as a child?

**DR:** I was never what you'd call an avid reader. I did read, but I did a lot of other things as well. I drew a lot, did a bit of dancing, I did a bit of music, I played the piano for many years. I do remember doing a project on Mexico at school and I put a lot of work into that though I did eventually go to Mexico some time later. I think there was a seed of adventure there but the business about going to university was just about having a bit of space to myself, to get on with my own life the way that I wanted to. I mean, parents of that generation were a bit different from parents now, they did expect you to do

pretty much what they thought you should do. To be honest, I would have preferred to go to art college. I didn't particularly want to go to university. I did that more to please my parents than to please myself.

**Gutter:** What did you study?

**DR:** English and Philosophy. But I wasn't a great student. I was quite young and immature. I could have done with another couple of years before studying, a sixth year, a gap year even but we didn't have gap years in those days. We didn't have gap years in those days. I actually think it makes quite a difference to people if they just wait a bit longer and think more about what they want to do. I was still trying to work out how to wash my clothes and learn to cook and do all these basic things. And, you know, the emotions of a teenager are pretty weird. I don't think I took the best from my studies. But I survived. I wasn't writing then.

**Gutter:** Did you have a clear idea of what you wanted to do when you graduated?

**DR:** I did want to travel and I did manage to do a little bit of travelling after I finished my degree. And then, of course, I ran out of money and I came back. So I didn't do the bigger travelling until a bit later after I had taken my teacher training course. I didn't have a clear idea of what I wanted to do for work. I didn't actually want to teach.

**Gutter:** Did you teach secondary?

**DR:** For a bit, but I didn't feel ready for it. I didn't feel cut out for it. I enjoy working with young people and continued my early days as a writer by going into schools quite a lot and I enjoyed that, but I didn't like the fact that we had to exercise discipline. English is a compulsory course so a lot of what you were doing was not teaching but about control.

**Gutter:** What came first, poetry or short stories?

**DR:** Poetry. I did begin writing some pretty God-awful stuff when I was at school, and I did read poetry at that time, and my mother bought me poetry books. There was a shop near the art school, I can't remember its name, that sold lots of little poetry pamphlets from all over. There was Tom Leonard's Six Glasgow poems alongside publications from Eastern Europe or Vietnam. I had Tom Leonard's first little six Glasgow poems from there.

**Gutter:** So you started writing poetry?

**DR:** I started writing poetry in my teens. It was a kind of odd situation in that I didn't begin writing again properly until my late twenties. I'd been travelling quite a lot before that. I'd been away from home in the States, in Mexico, and I'd written this dreadful travelogue, which I subsequently burned. But I was also drawing a lot while I was there. Somewhere or other the drawings that I did were stolen...

**Gutter:** An event mentioned in *Pelmanism*.

**DR:** Yes. There are some connections in *Pelmanism*. I think it was that sense of wanting something that I could reproduce easily, so that the original wasn't the most important thing. I was quite footloose at that point, unsettled. So I began writing poetry. I joined a writers' group – a women's writers' group – in Edinburgh. I stayed with that for about five years. It was a useful place for me at the time. I began to write short stories around that time too, but it's odd, you get used to a certain length. At first there was a wall of two

or three pages. Then I got beyond it.

**Gutter:** Were you using the criticism of others in the group, or were you using your own reading as the backbone, in terms of getting better and developing your voice?

**DR:** Well, I was living with Brian [the writer Brian McCabe] then, and he was already writing. I got some useful feedback from people in the group up to a point. I think my reading definitely mattered to me. How much it influences you is always an interesting question. I'm not sure that you necessarily want to be aware of a direct influence. I read a lot of work from Latin America at that point, not particularly magical realism but other things. As you say, it's another world.

**Gutter:** Central European writing too?

**DR:** Yes, and Central Europe too. Central European poetry particularly.

**Gutter:** I adore the absurdist responses to totalitarianism.

**DR:** There's a playfulness, there's a seriousness, there's an engagement with ideas, there's a slant.

**Gutter:** There's lot of humour in your short stories. Although it's impossible to draw any dominant threads or themes, one thing, particularly in the early collections, that stands out is sharpness. An unflinching attitude towards looking at the bad as well as the good. It's something that I admire in a lot of my favourite short story writers. Dare I say a kind of viciousness mixed with empathy makes the work utterly compelling? Where do you think that came from?

**DR:** I think I was a very critical young person, I was very critical of the world, of the people around me, of myself. I think that kind of refusal to say that everything's okay compelled me to look at the other side... and growing up has a dark side. I'm drawn to the dark side, perhaps more so than now... [pauses] No, I don't think that's true actually. I think it's a balance. It's always about both sides. Humour is important but the more I read of darker subjects, it needs humour to be accessible.

**Gutter:** I was talking about that with a debut writer yesterday, the importance of humour 'leavening the bread'...

**DR:** Exactly. You need the contrast in order to see what you really want to look at.

**Gutter:** In terms of that interest in the dark, do you think that was just a writer's sensibility, being interested in ambiguity and negativity in the light and the dark, or was there more to it? The times you were living in or a reaction to your upbringing?

**DR:** It's usually a combination of things. I don't think there's any one reason why I went the way I did in writing and I don't think I've ever had any sort of deliberate idea before I start something that I want to write. I often don't know what I'm writing until I've got it done. I tend to throw myself into a piece, often as an experiment.

**Gutter:** What comes first, voice or the idea?

**DR:** It depends. I mean, usually something very small. The piece I'm working on at the moment, which I'm really keen to get back to soon before it eludes me, flies off, started from the title. It was just a word. I was just so taken with the word that something stayed there, I don't know really at the moment what the story is but I know there's a story there.

**Gutter:** Do you think that's partly your poet's eye, because poetry can come out of the smallest thing, whereas, the received wisdom is that short stories and prose don't as much?

**DR:** For me, the story can come from a small idea... it's not so much a small idea, but something always seems to be given, something presents itself. As you say, it can be a voice, it can be a phrase, it can be watching somebody go by on the street. It can be a word. And when that thing is given, it's up to me to do something with it. I think it's the challenge of not knowing that keeps me going as a writer. I do not plan ahead that much, even with novels, which can be problematic. But it's that idea that I don't know whether I can do it or not, whether I can pull it off, that keeps me going, rather than the idea that, okay I've written so many stories before, I can do this fine.

**Gutter:** Each problem is a new challenge?

**DR:** Yes. One hopes to come to something with more in the way of skills and acquired confidence but there's still the risk that it won't work. I'm not a gambler with money, but maybe I am a gambler in that sense. I don't actually go back and look through earlier work that often. Very occasionally I'll go back and look at something and think – can I still do this? Did I do it then? But I know that when I began writing I tended to have things that I needed to write about. There were things that I had to get off my chest. So the earlier stories are perhaps a lot more about women, women's roles and women's experience. I'm not saying that's not important to me now, but I don't particularly want to stay in the same area.

And I also think that in terms of style, in terms of structure, the short story's a great place to try out different things. You can take risks that might be much bigger risks with a novel. You can afford to make mistakes, you can afford for things not to work.

**Gutter:** Have you used short stories as a means of coming to terms with things that have been happening to you, or is it much more of an intellectual exercise for you?

**DR:** I think there has to be something personal at stake, some kind of emotional question. Not necessarily a personal emotion or a personal experience, but there has to be something that matters to me, otherwise I'm not going to go there. That's why I don't find myself drawn to, although I can admire, very elaborate writing, game playing. The post-modern. I can admire it but often it leaves me cold.

**Gutter:** There needs to be an emotional centre to a story? A truth revealed?

**DR:** Yes, although at the same time, emotional content has to be treated with a certain level of distance, care and control.

**Gutter:** Would you say that one of the many differences between short stories and novels is that by nature, because a novel is such a great project, that emotional distance is inherent in the process? Because you're working over such a long time and the writer's own personal emotion dissipates, whereas you can write a short story in a couple of days whilst the emotion is still fresh...

**DR:** That's an interesting comment. I think it is probably the case. I've not really thought deeply about that, because I don't

think deeply about my own writing. I have to think more about other people's writing because I teach. But I think that's right. The longer you spend on something, you just couldn't stay in that emotional rubble for any length of time. Even if a piece started off as something that had some kind of connection to me, it would start to become something else quickly, and has to.

**Gutter:** You are very versatile, and you've undertaken some really interesting collaborations in opera and music and art. Do you still draw?

**DR:** I go to life drawing classes and I absolutely love them. I've been going for about three years and, to me, it's a different space to go in my head. I don't really care that much about the results, although of course you do care a little bit all the time, and you want praise from the teacher, but it's a useful concentration of the mind. The model's quiet, the model's concentrating, you're concentrating, it's surprisingly hard work.

**Gutter:** Do you think you have a real, compelling need to be creative all the time? Does a sense of frustration build up if you don't find an outlet?

**DR:** Yes it definitely does. There are times where I simply can't write because I have too much else to do, and I start to get quite crotchety, difficult to be around. The older I get, the less easy I find it is to take holidays and do nothing. I don't want to do nothing, I want to go and do something. I don't necessarily think of everything I do as being creative, I don't mind pottering about in my garden and also I swim quite a bit, which is extremely monotonous, but I get a lot of good ideas when my mind shuts down and I think it's important to rest the mind.

**Gutter:** Some call it active meditation, being involved in a repetitive physical action whether that be painting a fence or swimming.

**DR:** I can feel the mind going. I remember talking about the wall you break through, where you go through a barrier and the mind has gone somewhere else. You get that with swimming. I always know I've got to keep going, I'm not there yet.

**Gutter:** One of the things that sprinters talk about is that they need to relax as they run, and it's about being relaxed leading to absolute power.

**DR:** Not actually thinking about what you're doing. I really do the same thing in a different form...

**Gutter:** In the earlier stage of your career – those first ten or fifteen years and the publication of your first poetry and stories – did you see yourself as predominantly a short story writer because you had three story collections published one after the other? Or did you always perceive yourself as being a multi-faceted writer?

**DR:** Well, the first book of stories came out in the same year as the first collection of poetry, and obviously I'd been working on both alongside each other for quite a while. I became very, very keen on the short story and I became a little, not disillusioned with poetry, but I wasn't particularly keen on the poetry world at the time.

**Gutter:** In what sense?

**DR:** I don't know, I may have been wrong, but when I was writing both, the impression I got from some poets at the time was, 'Poetry is the highest form of writing, and you're almost betraying us by writing fiction as well', and I just couldn't be bothered with that. I just thought, 'well, okay, I'm not going to write poetry for a while', and actually at some point, foolishly said, 'I've tired of poetry', or something to that effect. And then I became interested in poetry again, and I just went back into it. But I tend to try not to push it, so if something presents itself I let it run. Which is why I've got a half book of poems at the moment, three quarters of a book of stories and another novel just about complete.

**Gutter:** Do you know instantly whether something is a poem when it comes to you, or if it's a short story?

**DR:** Pretty quickly, yes. And also I think, what happens is that I get into a certain mode for a while. Another poem will present itself, and then another, and then something else will happen. So rather than being very diligent and saying, okay, I must keep going with these poems, I must finish this book now, I don't, because writing is one of the few places where I have the chance to do it my way. In your job you have everybody else's deadlines and everybody else's expectations and so I am quite selfish in that respect and not very practical. If I feel like writing poems I'll try and do that. It does make for this odd situation though, where I've got various things unfinished.

**Gutter:** Do you think you resisted writing a novel at the time? Because I would imagine that there was a degree of pressure from your publishers [Secker and Warburg] to do that.

**DR:** Well, there wasn't initially

because after the first book was published, somewhere between the first and the second book, I won a prize in a short story competition, the Macallan, so they were quite happy to publish the next one, but then it became more difficult.

**Gutter:** Is that when you switched to Headline?

**DR:** Yes, and [Rose's editor at the time] Robin Robertson moved to Cape at that point. He's a very good editor. I, foolishly perhaps, held out for the short story. Commercially it's difficult. It's difficult for publishers. I do understand that. For me, with short stories, there's that chance to get it absolutely right, which there isn't so much with a novel.

**Gutter:** You've talked before about the opportunity for perfection in a short story in a way that that's never attainable in a novel, is that one of the things that particularly draws you to it?

**DR:** Well, I feel a little bit hesitant about saying that... I don't know that I really do think that, but it is more of a perfectionist art than the novel is, because there are usually parts of the novel where you just have to say, okay, this is as good as I can get it, and to move it on. Ideally, a novel has the potential, perhaps, to have every word in the right place, but you might only write one in your life.

**Gutter:** A short novel?

**DR:** A short novel, yes.

**Gutter:** So in terms of that switch from Secker to Headline, was it as simple as Secker's need for a novel?

**DR:** No, it was more complicated than that, and it was a question of an editor moving as much as anything. I can't remember what stage the novel was at, I really can't, whether the novel was something I'd been writing at the same time as the third story collection...

**Gutter:** *Pest Maiden*?

**DR:** Yes. When the idea for that presented itself it was an idea that needed the length. So I had to wrestle with it for a few years.

**Gutter:** A novel soaked in blood...

**DR:** Blood products...

**Gutter:** What was the starting point? A desire to respond emotionally to the litany of health scares that has occured over the proceeding fifteen years, or was it more than that?

**DR:** Yes but it was also the metaphorical nature of blood and the connections there. While I was writing it there was another scare, somewhere very similar to the place that this fictional story happens. And I suppose, there were all those things happening. It's the growth of science, things getting out of hand, things becoming uncontrollable. But it was also a story. It's difficult for me to say now what the initial spark of it was, because I can't remember. But, there always has to be some kind of non-literal level to your interest, because I think as soon as you start thinking about the actual thing, like the *Bodywork* poems, they're about the physical body but they can't *just* be about that, otherwise it doesn't interest me enough.

**Gutter:** The need for layers of meaning? Opportunities for multiple interpretation?

**DR:** Yes, but I think that's what we do with artists. Whatever art form they're interested in, this isn't just a painting of a woman, or, if it is, then it's a bit limited. There's usually something else going on.

**Gutter:** The lead character in *Pest Maiden* is Russell Fairley. He's a kind of everyman. For you, was he a an expression of society's loss of control, of its hypochondria, it vulnerability, in the face of HIV and AIDS, Mad Cow Disease and other blood-borne diseases?

**DR:** Yes although there was another thing that interested me in his character. There's a sub-plot, the idea that he thinks he's being made into a character in somebody else's novel, and it was really the rage that, in a way, kept him going for me. The world was doing things that he could not control, and he didn't like it, but he also didn't like the way he was being presented. Now that's something that I think is interesting. We see this kind of stuff happening in all sorts of different ways. I mean, I really don't like social media. I'm on Facebook but I never use it. It's being used as a weapon against people, you know, tweets and trolls, and all this kind of thing. And I think troll is a great name for these people, a fantastic name. But it seems like such a bizarre activity, people spend their life trying to get at complete strangers in this way. The virtual world can cause people real pain.

**Gutter:** With your prose writing, do you enjoying donning new personas and inhabiting other personalities?

**DR:** I did. I think, when I first began to experiment with using persona I found it quite liberating, and challenging as well. I stepped out of my shoes and tried to work to create a convincing character who didn't speak the same way as I did, who didn't think

the same was I did, and had them narrate their own story. I do that a bit less these days. It's not really a conscious decision, but I perhaps tried to get at the story, but from a different angle. I think if you write fiction, you have to be able to imagine the world from another point of view. I mean, ultimately, as a writer, you are going to infect everybody with your own hang-ups and your own attitudes. There's part of you that cannot help but be in there somewhere.

For me, writing is a way of trying to make sense of the world. I'm not trying to say this is good or bad, but it's for me to try to work out what makes people tick. And the only way I can do that is to try to get deeply into characters. Try to get inside them. People often ask where your characters come from and I found that it was important not to base a character too closely on somebody I knew, because you've already got this huge history, but to make a character from real-life details, and combine them and change them. I worked a lot from a painter friend's paintings which are imaginary portraits, because I always saw stories in there.

**Gutter:** How long did it take to write *Pelmanism*?

**DR:** Difficult question because I was doing other things as well. I probably started it around 2009 and I certainly finished it a couple of years ago. It was slow to appear.

**Gutter:** Between *Pest Maiden* and *Pelmanism*, one can see significant progression. It's really stunning. Although, by nature, it's about very different themes, you've written it in a very different way, and one can feel the craft that's developed over twenty years of short story writing. It's not a lyrical book, but there is a poet's eye in the detail, and it's a real pleasure to read. Did you choose to write a more – and this isn't a pejorative word – mannered book? A mixture of sadness and beauty.

**DR:** It was a very different story to *Pest Maiden*. I think, structurally, I found myself wanting to create it as more of a mosaic, so that each section has got some sense of its own identity. Very short sections. So that it's not so much a linear narrative, more of a building block effect. It's not plot driven, but then very little I write is plot driven. I was creating these short sections and wanted them to have a sense of completion. I like reading from it because the sections can work on their own without too much explanation. And I think it's maybe easier to get that sense, if it's lyricism we're talking about, when you're writing in short sections. Or, at least, I find it easier.

**Gutter:** Was *Pelmanism* a product of having written so much about family, and family dynamics, and the vagaries of family life, within your short stories? Did it feel like the logical place to go with the novel, in terms of continuity?

**DR:** I suppose so. Again it was a story that I wanted to deal with and maybe I write too much about family.

**Gutter:** I don't think you can write too much about family.

**DR:** The novel I'm working on at the moment is not about family.

**Gutter:** It's historical? About blasphemy and religious belief? How far are you?

**DR:** Quite far. Towards the end.

**Gutter:** Does it frustrate you that poetry and short stories are such uncommercial activities?

**DR:** It makes it difficult. It makes it difficult for the publishers as much as it makes it difficult for me. You know, why should things be commercial? I mean, I don't know that poetry was ever a hugely commercial business but it didn't stop people writing it. I think it would be a real shame if it became so difficult to publish that we didn't have any. Because there are people who do enjoy reading it. There are fewer than those who enjoy blockbusters but, that's the way of life. I think, in the ideal world, there should be room to satisfy a whole range of different reading tastes, rather than just what sells a lot. But I know that it's a difficult world and I think, unfortunately, what's going to happen is that it's going to be harder and harder to sell things which aren't commercial.

**Gutter:** You're director of the creative writing distance learning programme at the University of Edinburgh. Over and above the enjoyment of helping writers improve, do you draw any sustenance yourself from editing other people's work, or is it a job?

**DR:** It's a very hard job. As you say, I enjoy seeing people's work grow. I enjoy working with the students that are all over the world, literally. But, in terms of my own work, I have to find my own place. I think it's quite important to try to make a break between that and what I'm doing as a teacher. Just to get away and find my own space, and write and then come back, because when I'm teaching it's pretty all-encompassing. It's long hours, it's intense and, you're giving out quite a lot of your own creative energy to other people's work. Is the question do I learn anything from my students? It's a complicated question. I've been teaching a long time. I think one thing I probably do gain from it is that, because we give quite a lot of detailed feedback to students, you do become very aware of common errors. So I would hope that I don't fall into the trap of making these common errors myself. I also think that I do have to practise what I preach, and that means, you know, take a bit more time, give a piece of work the attention it needs. These kinds of obvious things. But in terms of the creative side of things, I don't tend to discuss with a student what their plans are. That's not a lot of use to me and I don't think I'm very good at talking about something in the abstract, I'm much better when there's something there. Talking about strategies to go on with it and develop it.

**Gutter:** You've collaborated with artists across a range of disciplines, in opera, in non-operatic music, you've worked with artists. What do you get from these partnerships that's different from the rest of your creative life? And is there anything that you haven't done yet that you'd like to do?

**DR:** I just recently finished a song cycle, which I'd always wanted to do. It was with Red Note and the singer Karen Cargill, who's a wonderful singer, and the composer is Rory Boyle, whom I worked with on *Kasper Hauser*. So I'm really pleased that that happened.

**Gutter:** How did the *Kasper Hauser* libretto come about?

**DR:** The composer was given a Creative Scotland Award. It was written specifically for emerging voices so it was sung by the final year opera students at, what was the RSAMD, now the Conservatoire. Rory said that there weren't a lot of parts for younger voices, and I don't know enough about the technicalities, but you have to grow into certain roles. When you write the words, and somebody writes the music, and then you hear it being sung and you see people acting the part, it's incredible, for me, to see where things can go without me. Writing for the page, the control freak in me comes out quite quickly. But when it's something that's written for somebody to sing, I start to very quickly take a back seat.

**Gutter:** Is that liberating in terms of not having that responsibility?

**DR:** It's not so much about not having responsibility, because I still have responsibility for the text. It's just really exhilarating to see where those words can go, the transformation between the words on the page to them being sung. And *Kaspar Hauser* is a dark, sad, sad story, and there were a lot of tears in the audience that night, and I was crying, and I'm not usually that affected by my own writing. But it wasn't about the writing, it was about the singing. Working with musicians is really enjoyable in that respect.

**Gutter:** Is there anything else that really attracts you, in terms of a similar kind of collaboration? Have you got anything in the pipeline?

**DR:** I know that a dance company did some work based on my *Bodywork* poems, which I unfortunately missed as I was away. I think it was a fairly liberal interpretation, but that's fine. I would have loved to have seen it. I think I'd possibly like to do a bit more collaboration with scientists, because I really enjoyed the neuroscience collaboration I did. I'd also like to write another opera, and I know what I'd like to write it on but I'm not going to say.

# Works (Portraits)

*Dan Spencer*

1.

Here, he sits on the floor with his knees bent and his hands on his knees. One knee (his left) touches the floor and the other knee (the right) is raised. His hands are on his knees, the elbows bent. He's arranged his elbows, knees and hands into specific positions, creating a recognisable pose which can't be called kneel, crouch, squat, cross-legged, lotus, half-lotus or anything else.

He leans forward. He looks oversized. The frame is like a box into which he has crammed his large naked body. The head, in particular, is very far forward, very large and intent. (But it's a self-portrait, so of course it's himself at whom he's looking so intently).

Have I remembered his hands correctly? One hand may be on the floor. It may be holding a paintbrush, as if he's in the process of painting this picture of himself. Is he left-handed or right-handed? He has grey eyes. The painting is the size of a fireplace. It stands on the floor, standing against the wall, like a fireplace.

2.

Or, here, he's standing. He's in the role of Saint Sebastian. The painting is the size of a door, and it stands at the top of the stairs like a door, with the artist standing in the picture like a man standing in a doorway. The chin is tilted upwards and the eyes look up. He holds his hands behind his back and his legs are bent slightly. 'You've done yourself some favours,' we tell him. 'If anything, I made it smaller,' he says. Naturally, his penis interests us greatly.

But why a saint? Why arrows? He's shot full of them. He radiates arrows. I shouldn't care. He can paint himself how he likes. It isn't him I'm looking at, when I look at him.

3.

And there's a sculpture of a woman (the head and torso and arms). The clay is a light, pine colour. The eyes are closed and the breasts are quiet. The head is dropping to one side. The top of the head has been sliced clean off, to fit the kiln. The flat top is tempting. I want to stand a plant pot there. I think she's his lover.

His lover is an older woman. She's in the dining room, painting with watercolours. On the table is a dead goldfish. Her son is unhappy. He doesn't want to be here with his mother's lover. I'm unhappy. I don't want to be here with her son. She's unaware. She's looking closely at the fascinating, bright anatomy of the dead goldfish.

Did he make the sculpture or did she? Is the sculpture really of her, or a studio model? On the walls are line drawings of women. Who drew them? I don't ask. If I asked, he'd tell me. If I write, 'Is the sculpture his lover?' he'll read it and say yes or no, or he'll say, 'You were right about that part but wrong about this.' I don't want to know. I don't want it touched.

4.

The landscapes and the weather pictures are also done on portrait canvases. As a young man he paints English fields with muddy greens and mustard yellows, and rainy skies with greys and whites. He likes paint. His skies are heavy with it. His landscapes are stormy. His storms are landscapes. When he's older, he paints lakes and mountains with a palette knife. The hill is mint-green. The water is lilac and white and grey and blue...

He's the painter I like most. He's as good as Turner, it seems. Obviously, that's not right. He's an unknown. But I see every artist in the light of him – Rembrandt, Pollock, Freud... He colours everything. When I talk about art, I wait for him to agree. We walk around a gallery. We know how to talk about art. I listen in on conversations, thinking better thoughts than anyone.

5.

*The painting of his father.* It's done years after his father has died. His mother says, 'It doesn't look like him,' which seems hurtful. Maybe both of them feel hurt (the mother and son), because of how close the painting gets them to the dead husband or father, or how far away it leaves them, because of how much it does or doesn't look like him.

Another time, out of nowhere, he says to me, 'My father had died by the time I was your age.' I'm working at the college this year. I'm not in his department but to be near him I go to his office. He doesn't say more. I'm surprised. Where did that come from? I'm almost amused. I'm flippant. Why can't I be kinder?

6.

Then: photography. 'Recently I'm not painting,' he says. 'I'm teaching a lot of photography on the timetable. This is the first year I haven't taught any art lessons.' It's the year he retires. Photography interests him – the mechanics and chemistry. He likes finding the right aperture and shutter speed. He likes the darkroom work. 'I like DIY,' he says. 'I like building picture frames more than painting pictures.' He builds a good fence. Into cement he sinks a good post, well-levelled, well-spaced.

7.

But when his mother dies, he says, 'Life is a holiday,' and I feel bleak. 'I'm going to see her body a second time,' he says. 'You can come if you'd like.' Does he want me to come? I don't go. We visit a gallery and talk about art. It doesn't work.

We go into her flat. I look around at things: the pantry curtain; Vermeer's milkmaid, faded and greenish; the sheepskin rug. Standing on the TV is a drawing of his brother. They don't talk – the artist and his brother. They fell out over the divorce. He did the drawing as a young man. His brother was young. It's tenderly done. A few lines. A glance. A wave of hair.

8.

I find him painting. Maybe I've intruded. We stand together looking at it. It's another landscape on a portrait canvas. We talk about the contrasts with the hills and lakes, or with the cloud and sky. He wonders if parts could be lightened or darkened. I think, yes, he could work on some of it. Sometimes, turning a painting upside-down shows how well it holds together. But, having stepped back, he doesn't want to start up again, so this one's finished.

# Sol's a choreographer

*Colin Herd*

His latest piece is designed to really get his own back on his former partner Tim. Premiering at the Southbank thanks to his friendship with Dominic, with music performed by the incomparably exquisite London Sinfonietta and composed by Luke ('No-Headed Nightingale') Bedford, the piece is called 'Domestic'.

There's a fridge on one side of the stage. A Smeg. On the other, there's a stainless steel splashguard, a sink, some cupboards. Between them, an island hob. Adjacent to that there's a beech table, and six Hans Wegner Wishbone Chairs. Simply laid, with edgy studio plates, a taupe cloth, Arne Jacobsen cutlery. This stuff's actually been salvaged from Sol's flat, which is on the market.

Not exactly a sell-out. But Jude Kelly's here. And Judith Mackrell, Zoe Anderson and Ian Palmer. The poet Steven Fowler. The artist Charlie Billingham, whose exhibition 'Hunting Dogs and Hunting Cats' just ended.

When the lights go, Dominic and Sol turn to smile at one another, thud rather than chink their plastic lager cups. They're old school friends, from just outside Richmond. Dominic points to the second page: 'the characters are entirely the products of the choreographer's imagination, and have no relation to any person in real life.' Sol laughs. Lifts his palm up to his mouth in mock 'oops'.

Dancer 1 breezes in with shopping bags. He's dressed tightly in black. Looks like he has a lot on his mind, beginning with flowers, under his arm. He puts the bags on the counter by the splashguard and takes a pair of scissors from a knife block. He zips them up the cellophane then takes off the elastic band. He fetches a ribbed glass vase from one of the cupboards, turns the tap on and fills it halfway full. He cuts each stem individually before putting them in. Mostly tulips. A few Irises. A twig or two. A slapdash arrangement.

He takes it to the table, turns and makes long strides back towards the island, where he picks up a wooden chopping board. He lifts out and unwraps a chicken. Smears it with oil. Cuts a lemon in half. Puts it in the cavity, both halves. He stops as though he hears something, then carries on. Grinds salt and pepper all over the chicken, and in the cavity.

It's been silent till now but at this point he takes his phone out of his pocket and slots it into a music system, selects something.

Strings begin to swell, fairly quietly at first, a subtle and varied sequence of bleebs and echoes. Chaotic, disordered and charged. As I understand it, the piece is partly inspired by Hugue Dufort, in turn inspired by Brueghel.

The chicken gets put in the top oven. Dancer 1's dramatically washing spinach, with his hands. Taking clumps and just rinsing them through the violent stream. It's one of those giraffe neck taps, craning like a droopy flower. Eventually, he lifts the bag, shoves the nozzle in and grasps tightly so that it blows up like a balloon. He shakes it about then carefully drains out the water and puts it all in a pan.

He goes to the fridge and takes out a glass tart case with pastry already laid out in it. He pricks the base all over with a fork and stretches out some brown paper to lay across. Gets some ceramic beans from the cupboard and tosses a handful in.

This goes in another oven. Bedford's piece is at odds with the quiet scale of the dance so far. During the journey to the fridge to get the tart there was a percussive double bass portion played by Enno Seft but we're back to viola at the minute, bewildering and ravishing.

While Dancer 1 is getting blackberries out of the fridge, Dancer 2 appears at the left of the stage. Looks sleepy, but doesn't do a comic pantomime arms-stretch or anything, just limps kind of languidly across the room, straight to the fridge. So they meet beside the Smeg and have to maneuver around each other.

The movements of Dancer 1 are instantly more twitchy; heightened by the fact he starts whipping cream. Dancer 2 opens a can of Carlsberg, a moment that is underscored by silence from the Sinfonietta. 1's hand is getting tired, you can tell. But he carries on relentless, now swirling the whisk around in the bowl in circles, now just left to right in short jerks. It takes a while but it's definitely thickening, which you can tell by the way his facial expression changes depending on his reaction when he checks.

The score gets frenetic.

You start to wonder if he'll stop whipping in time. He doesn't exactly look like someone who instinctively knows when enough is enough. Eventually though, he puts the whisk and bowl down and, out of one of the shopping bags, takes a baguette. Breaks pieces off with his hands and puts them in a dish.

From the fridge, he gets some olives. 2 is still hovering around, finishing the can in large gulps. 1 shunts past him. As he goes to close the fridge, 2 puts his arm out to get another can. He leaves the empty on the table and walks out the door.

1 takes the baguette and olives to the table and reaches out a Copenhagen butter dish from the fridge. His posture's despondent, spent. He's still slackening off his stiff peaks arm by stretching and shaking it and letting it dangle down. He sits, toys with the can. The only movement on stage his gently swinging leg and his finger wavering on the ring pull.

By the time 2 comes back in, 1's still sitting there and 2 scoffs, mutters something under his breath, leaves another empty on the table and opens another can, with vigour so that it froths out on the top and he has to catch it with his lip.

It must be time for 1 to check the chicken but you can tell his enthusiasm has gone out of preparing this meal. Still, he presses on, lifting it out and up on to the counter top to rest. He goes out of the room. During this passage, where the stage is empty, it's the first really good opportunity to focus on Bedford's score: economical gestures and clear forms that convey immense resonance and depth, with a sort of mumblecore simplicity. The players of the Sinfonietta are in gorgeous cohesion, even as their instruments rasp and wheeze.

The pause lasts 4.5 minutes. During which period, I guess you're meant to be wondering who is going to return first. The surprise though is that they both re-enter together. 1 to the 'Alien' inspired sink to wash his hands, 2 to the fridge and then the table.

1's carving the bird, putting it on a sizeable platter, while at the same time steaming the spinach lightly and popping it into a serving bowl, both of which he carts off to the table as soon as they are done. He makes a last minute trip to the fridge to get an opened bottle of wine and a jar of Dijon mustard.

By the time he's back, 2 has some chicken, some bread, some olives and some spinach on his plate, so 1 can serve himself. During the meal, things seem to relax. The shoulders of each dancer slump a little and they appear to be talking, though Dancer 1 has his back to the audience and Dancer 2 is sort of in profile but angled so as not to be very visible.

Anyway, everything seems peaceful enough until suddenly without any warning, Dancer 1 visibly bristles. His shoulders stiffen and he puts down his fork. He gesticulates a bit, nothing crazy, but dancer 2 flips. Bangs his fists onto the table. He lifts up 1's wine glass and pours it over his food.

1 is in tears now; they've come on quite sudden. He shrinks away, actually moves his chair further down the table and has his head in his hands.

2 continues eating, sort of, pushing his food around his plate. Anyway, something suddenly twigs for 1. He panics, gets up and runs to the oven, which, when he opens it lets out a sigh of billowing smoke. 1's pissed off now, angry and upset. He's burnt the fucking tart case and ruined desert. He takes it over to the counter where it's clearly visible from the table.

2 laughs, enjoying the moment briefly. But then 1 obviously says something to the tune of blaming 2 for this latest mis-hap in their lives (insinuating that all the other mis-haps are his fault too.)

2 flips again and this time it's intense. He lifts up the table, still covered in all the dishes and food etc and just tosses it over with ease. So it's now on its back, its legs in the air.

1 looks taken aback if not surprised. He says 'no, please, no' and backs away behind the island hob. There then follows a comic chase around the hob which involves 1 grabbing the knife block when he goes passed because he knows what 2 will do if he spots them.

After a couple of circuits, 2 gives up the futile chase and picks up the still hot-ish tart case and lobs it straight at 1, who ducks. A couple of glasses follow, the bowl of cream, the blackberries.

1's just crouching now, covering his head. A big splodge of whipped cream falls down one of the cupboard doors on to the floor. 2 heads to the fridge and lays his hands on anything, wine bottles, soy sauce, sweet chilli, piccalilli, jam, mustard, etc, etc. Anything and everything he can find, he's hurling in a rage at 1, who is still just sitting there, protected by the island, covering his head.

After a couple of minutes, the fridge now almost empty, 2 suddenly looks wearied and pained, takes a beer from the fridge, opens it, then walks over to the counter, takes a cigarette from a packet and lights it. He goes to the table, picks up a chair, sits on it, facing away from 1.

1 leaps up, scrambles for his keys on the counter and runs off stage, leaving 2 just sitting there motionless, confused and bewildered, until the curtain goes down.

The score succulently falls apart, each player dropping out until you're left with a piano and a whining, breathless cello in discord.

'Domestic scale dance is the latest thing in choreography,' says The Guardian, 'the sort of dance we dread to do each day and don't even know we're doing it. Does for dance what 'Who's Afraid of Virgina Woolf?' did for theatre. But there's an unmistakable and unpalatable cruelty about 'Domestic'. The choreographer could learn something from the quiet thoughtfulness of playwright Sharman Macdonald.'

# The Collected History of Museums

*Martin MacInnes*

Gliding, the clerk settled into one continuous long movement, the automatic lifting of the left corner of his mouth seeming to tug his right arm upwards towards the scanner, leisurely gripping the hard black plastic, playing with it, at ease, reassuring the facing customer as to the naturalness of the procedure, the clerk standing there with a desk and monitor between them, holding in his right hand only the scanner, the long lead looping down under the desk.

The customer maintained her composure, moving slowly, turning her head around as if surveying not just the clerk but the desk, the windows behind, and in the other direction the remainder of the wide, dimly lit room. Along the front of the desk was a series of items put there for display; she looked at each of them in turn, considering her options, enjoying not yet speaking, thinking about several other things she hadn't thought about in some time.

He moved the scanner around the grip of his right hand, changing position apparently in reaction to the thing itself, as if it were unstable. He enjoyed the ease of his command, the leisure, the light sheen of sweat on the plastic material of the scanner and the fact that he hadn't done anything yet, hadn't said anything, that neither of them had.

They paused a little longer before beginning their interaction, though in truth they were each already adjusting their body in reaction to the one facing, moving as it did, anticipating the opening line and the response, the way it would all likely go from there; they ran their tongues across their lower teeth and breathed. In this preceding moment anything remained possible – they might even go off-script. The number of things to talk about being without limit. There were ways that they could go. There was the anxiety of the night, the mounting daily confusion, suspicious, regrets, and then pure curiosity. The movement of clouds invisible from here shifted the range of sunlight available from the window and dust-mites slowed the scene still further, the room appearing warm, clammy, discouraging any movement, making the clerk and customer feel desultory, bodies languid, minds not elsewhere but not here either. They let the silence aggregate. Palpably and not determined by either one of them, there was the suggestion that they might just as well give up. That it might be better to give up, freer and closer and less full of shame. The suggestion passed between them in the slow scene, damp, soft, silent, the attraction of being less full of shame, a course of action that might ease the ringing dullness in the head, the noise of monotony, the alarm of the defined world.

She placed her items on the desk, specifically the perspex verge meeting the black painted and varnished wooden counter. He was to inspect the items minimally and without intrusion, but first there was the task of deciding between them who was most to blame in having not yet spoken and yet still proceeding, as if it were not necessary yet that they should speak. Somewhere between abandoning it all and walking away and it never being the same again and, on the other hand, of briskly and adeptly moving on with the transaction was what was happening, and they were each to blame, neither of them yet having decided anything, and life still continuing marginally. She relaxed her shoulders which had an effect on him, his eyes becoming different in their proportions, his nostrils changing too. It had been several seconds, their being presented with each other. The dust faded from view again, and maybe that would be the lull over.

He didn't have any more to be, currently, than what he was in uniform standing two inches distant from his side of the desk, divided from the public part of the counter, his right arm poised and ready to begin, his eyes watching the new objects, his left arm moving only so far as to be making a gesture about gathering the objects and moving forward and processing them. He said hello, three seconds after her approaching the desk, she had appeared engaged in something else, he wasn't here to move her on, he should let her be, leave it up to her as to when to begin and to end the spoken part of the formality. He held the object, she thought, the scanner probably, as if it were interesting it was there though he was quite at ease with it, he liked it, she thought, and though he is supple with it part of the way he plays is as if almost to say he doesn't know anything about it, doesn't know what it is or how it works, he just has it, it's almost foreign as he controls it there, she thinks. He looks towards the things she's brought as he says hello with only a small opening of his mouth, a glance upwards towards her, a meeting, and she nods and smiles no more expansively and at last it's begun and now they are locked together in something impersonal that will take care of itself and they needn't even think. He expresses statements and question in a variety of acceptable ways, saying them like he carries the scanner, easy with them, having used them so many times they are almost a part of him, yet appearing also like a spectator, ignorant and mildly amused at the flow.

This is the time now of her waiting, the nine seconds of having nothing to do as he processes the transaction, scanning and tallying and checking and bagging, all in a manner designed to minimise her self-consciousness in having nothing to do, ducking strenuously as he whips air in to open the bag, doing all he can to make it clear to her that no-one is expecting her to do anything, no-one is observing her, and in doing all he can to minimise her self-consciousness he is amplifying his own, very much aware as he prises one thin white plastic bag from a block and lifts it and opens it a little then whips air in to inflate it so he can get the objects inside and complete things, but until then he couldn't be more present, to his chagrin, aware that she is watching him in his role, watching the way he does things, how adept or otherwise he is, wandering what he is thinking as he goes about these menial and routine tasks, because surely, she would think, he doesn't need to think about any of this, he could be thinking about anything, that would be one of the perks of the job, and surely she would be thinking, he thinks, if she knew, how vain and presumptive of him to imagine she is thinking about him, that she is even aware of him at all, because why would she be, why would she be thinking any of this?

Regarding one particular statement, she thinks, his manner suggests he is waiting to find out if he has not asked this of her already. That would be embarrassing. As he waits to find out, assuming for some reason that she would let him know he has blindly repeated himself, he hopes that if he has indeed done this then she will not think that he has been mocking her or mocking the idea of the transaction and the associated roles, that hasn't been what he is doing at all. Unintended repetitions simply happen sometimes, and he is as surprised to hear them as she is, perhaps more so. Sometimes he will think he has heard himself making those repetitions and he will cut himself down mid-stride, so to speak, not finishing the question and apologising for what he has already said too much, and then far from relieved the customer appears confused and he thinks maybe he has got it wrong, maybe he hasn't repeated himself, because how can he know, and anyway it has all gone on now for far too long, it should all have been over already.

She wonders if he will notice. Surely he will notice. He can't be *that* good an actor, though he's certainly one of the better ones she's worked with lately. He can't actually have made himself become so occupied within the role that he fails to observe what is actually going on during the encounter. If he has indeed noticed the identity of the object and is only pretending that he hasn't, then, she wonders, is that more or less impressive than not noticing in the first place? Which of the two, for one of them is surely applicable, constitutes the better performance?

She has gone off script in the choice of one of the objects, one of the things that she has brought over for him to process. When it becomes clear what the object is then they will either appreciate it wryly or she will be reprimanded for perceived frivolousness. Only those in the front three rows surrounding the stage might have a chance of reading the label on the object that she brought to him and placed on the public side of the counter eighteen seconds ago. She had practiced many times alone and with a stand-in object, not a real one, of course, though to effectively perform the role of a customer in a store she would have to get it out of her head that those objects were in any way rare or unusual, she would need to give the impression, to the audience in the museum and to the actor playing the clerk as well, in order not to detract from his performance, which would in turn adversely affect her own, that she lifted and carried and viewed such objects all the time, that it was no big deal at all, that she was actually quite at ease living within historical reconstruction because she didn't known it, she wanted them, as they watched her in re-enactments of old days, to forget, if only for a second, that none of this was real and to believe instead that this world was present and alive.

# Kingfisher

*Russell Jones*

I was in the 39 degree winter of Kochi.
The water was sleeping,
we were riding on its dream.

Suddenly, led by the changing shadows,
he flashed through the warm breeze,
plummeted into that second world.

He had barely left me
but his dive filled the river.
Not a drop of movement on the surface
but his image hung, ablaze,

his wings like cloaks of energy.
His tail was a bolt of topaz.
His beak was sunlight, mango, flame.
His feet were origami

folded from the backwaters of India
and in his hunter's eyes precision shone.
In the silence, in the centre
of the season he was a vein,

a quick beating rhythm.
He came back empty
but time snapped

and was reborn
in his dance

of light and fire and ice.

# Oruru

*Robert James Berry*

means owl.

In the far north
where big rivers run hard
where the sun bubbles like a kettle

our road bakes in peculiar light.
Dust storms when a wagon trundles by.

The Swamp Palace cinema
a converted barn
showed its last flick in 1947 –

in its roof trees
under a round moon
owls roost.

There is never rain.
Only drought.

We wash our crockery
in old bath water

cows stumble from sunstroke,
about a cracked earth.

But the owls, moon-eyed,
sleek from killing
can be heard come dusk.

They are a chorus: *oruru.*

# Call of the corncrake

*Jim Carruth*

No beauty in my voice
rough-throated and guttural
ratchet tongue that calls to you
from the edge of the harvest
coarse, insistent yet invisible
to your disinterested eye.

Don't wait on future's silent field
to trigger false sentiment
a cheap lament for the long gone
Switch your engine off, seek me
my song, my small speckled body
my short walk in the sun.

# Werewoods

*Susan Haigh*

When mist poured along potato drills
when murkwebs hung from every branch,
the forest floor was borage blue
and gorse-and-bumble-bee gold.

Today, I see the woods are safe.
Bears and wolves that watched
in fog and moved among trees,
just out of sight, caught
with the tail of my eye,
have gone to caves and lairs.
Beside me, a werewolf
trots along, noses my hand,
nowhere near as were as he was.

# Pavie

*Fran Baillie*

Alangside the cashline,
lehin on the pavie,
ootside the uni,
somebiddy's bairn;
hameless,
nameless,
lost aathin.
Barkit, mankit, mingin,
sarcophagust in auld cardboard
dowpie atween roostie fingrs,
ehz barricaydit agin the world,
bony dug flechin.

Beggin fir cheenge
hopin fir cheenge.

# from a diary found in the rubbish– not serialised in any newspaper

*Jim Ferguson*

2$^{nd}$ *august*

morning: no mail
nothing but sad times

fuckwit this
fuckwit that
fuckwit the other

thats whit this *is*
thats whit is *is*
thats whit that *is*

its aw the fuckin *is-ness*
ah know who am ur
ah know the fuckin lotta yeez

5$^{th}$ *august*

morning: no mail
nothing but sad times

baith reading n writin
the diary uv a lunatic
n the journal uv a nutter

who the fuck izit
some cunts alter ego?
that aw depends -

cummings n the gone
n that wummin fielding
no fa-fuckin-nella

that daft fuckin diary
whits hur fuckin name
thinks shiz middle aged

but it izny fuckin hur
n shiz only aboot thurty
n thin then fat n thin again

*13th august*

morning: no mail
nothing but sad times

aw worried
aw the time aboot
items deeply trivial

its no helen fielding
its e e cummings
thats who

*21st august*

morning: no mail
nothing but sad times

fuckin know whit it is
racked wae pain n numbness
cancered tae the sky

livir n lung
gets yi way down low
levels yi, right

doon tae the depths
bottom uv despair

*26<sup>th</sup> august*

morning: no mail
nothing but sad times

thats where its at
sittin in gods waitin room
waitin tae die

thats fuckin it
thats the fuckin thing
the thing that it is

that i wiz fuckwittin
talkin aboot,
christ, thatzgrim

- - -


evening: sky glorious
amazing pink and orange crescents
sun a yellow-white orb
huge, n low

– infinite and infinitesimal
feel infinite and infinitesimal

sense of sight sends a message
a soothing electric shock
let the nerves twitch quietly …

try tae walk into it
walk intae it …

# Definition of an Optimist:

*Wendy Miller*


One who opts
to see
through
the mist

Even if
being a Scot
your glass
has a habit
of lookin
half empty

you could always
fill it up but
fill it right up

dae-it!
dae-it!
dae-it!

# 'Likes'

*Ross Wilson*

Facebook 'selfies for cancer' inspired her
to empty a cupboard in her mum's kitchen,
photo the empty shelves, and post:
SHELFIES FOR FOODBANKS
with a link to send donations.

No one 'liked' it. Some were angry.
Cancer victims don't choose cancer!
Who did *she* know used food banks?
Why encourage charity for scroungers?
*They've* enough money for fags and drugs!

Her mum thought it a great lesson:
*never* discuss politics or religion
on Facebook or, well, anywhere *ever*.
Oh, remember the selfie you posted?
Remember all the 'likes' it generated?

No one wants to think about ugly things,
people want to see nice pretty things
like you, her mum explained, re-stocking
the shelves with tin after tin after tin,
then forcing the door shut, to keep them in.

# Nut Roast

*Christopher Barnes*

A zigzag-sprinkling head-dress,
worn for Hogmanay guzzling.

    *'The menu is well planned'*

Madge crinkles her beak,
retrieves peas.

    *'A table with ironed linen'*

Sag of cuff mops gravy.

    *'A welcoming host'*

Dropper-in smiling. Easy temper repartee,
humming for the clockface
as Angelina's Max Factor bloats
into anaphylactic shock.

    *'If you have only one oven'*

\*

New York Dining Suite
Includes Circular Glass Table & Four Chairs
13cm Circular Glass Table Top
Black Bonded Leather Chairs

# The House Of Illusions

*Christopher Barnes*

A lolloping baby girl heaves up stairs.

  *'Twiggy was born in North London'*

Rag doll guffaw, forget-me-not curls wobble
on hollow-bubble foreheads.

  *'Her Mod, Mod Teen World'*

Lobster-red bed, lemon butter curtains.

  *'Success epitomising the age'*

Two dressing altars with enthralled mirrors.

  *'An anti-fur campaigner'*

A clean-sweep, Miss.

  *'A skinny kid with the'*

Anything you itch for, ask.

\*

Clarins Paris
Capital Lumiere Jour
Soin Anti-Age Unifant – Toutes Peaux
Vital Light Day
Illuminating Anti-Aging Cream
All Skin Types

# hospital tea break

*Charlie Gracie*

the tiny space alive with smoke and the chat of women
*you don't get fucked when you're over fifty*
laughs, swigs of tea, long draws on fags
I focus on the floor, redden to the tune of their voices
*Ah think Ah've become a virgin again*
eyes burn into my head

I can feel their sweat, inhale it with the smoke, slurp it with my tea
sweet sweat, worked up in a morning of lifting and changing and feeding
makes me want to be a woman, to laugh like this, talk dirty, embarrass the laddie
when I rise to go, maternal instincts bubble through the fug
*we chasing you out, son?*
silence as I click the door behind me
then laughter, warm and soft
soft as a mammy's knee

# Billy the Rig

*A P Pullan*

*for B.M., abseiler, Delta Rig, Brent Field.*

I think of Billy out there
stuck in that tube of a rig's leg,
lagged by a full North Sea.

What if its foot inches into the shaft
made by those fathom long bits?
Billy lowering through the mantle

like a plumb of lead to be smelt.
Some days I have him sat in its toe
bridie in one hand, the other tapping

with the back of his spoon
awaiting news from nearby rigs or silent,
save for the odd yawn and stretch

as a seam folds then settles.

# Threads From A Dying Village

*Tom Pow*

### The Choice

When she fell pregnant, they arranged to meet. She thought in the village; he thought on the road. Because of the dangers that stood in their way at that time, there was no going back. He waited till morning, then took what the road had to offer. After many years, he returned, a rich man. You could say, it was like a fairy tale. But she became nervous, when he struck up a friendship with her son. Look, he said to calm her, all these years ago, I had nothing to give you at the end of the road. But our son could have whatever he wants. And that is what scares me, she said. For I wanted nothing. You see, all those years ago, I made no mistake when I stayed in the village. He nodded. Then let our son make the same choice, between the everything you did not want and the nothing you so clearly desired.

### Comings and Goings

There had come to be so many empty houses in the village, they were relieved when one of them was occupied again. Silence had surrounded their marriage for so long, it was refreshing to live next to a house with so many comings and goings. The girls – though some were considerably older than girls - were bussed over from the nearby border. There was only a handful of their words the old couple could understand. But, after all, a greeting is a greeting in any language. Sometimes, on summer nights, they'd hear one of the girls put on an act: her moans filled the stillness of their room, like something wild that had found its way in there and was looking for a way out.

What's that noise? his wife would say.

He'd smile and reply, Why, that used to be you, my dear. And quite properly, each time, she'd slap him.

When a house was found closer to the city, where the girls would be paid more, the house in the village lay empty again. The old couple lay each night in the silence, apart from the occasional bark, a distant car. The old man smiled, when he recalled those nights the sounds of love – or something he mistook for the sounds of love - had settled over them again, in the way of a cat, once abandoned, that had found its way back home.

### Souvenirs

There was an old woman whose mother had been brought up in the Pale, the settlement established by Catherine the Great for Russian Jews. Whenever pogrom threatened, the family moved to another settlement. To the woman's mother, the village was an idea, portable, depending on a few symbolic and practical possessions. Her father, on the other hand, had come from a village in Scotland which held to the myth that whoever passed under a particular bridge would not return. (As she was telling me this, I could see the bridge – one of those with a low arch and a damp, muddy puddle below it that never quite clears.) It was conscription that prised her father from the village and brought him together with the refugee who would become his wife. Their daughter had a love of travel all of her life. She kept a cabinet stocked with souvenirs. But, if you asked her, she would be unable to tell you much about any of them.

### The Larder

When she woke from her sleep, she saw him in the kitchen, through the half open door, tip the pan of boiling water till some fell over the spine of the cat. The cat screeched and ran out of the door. He had always been a deliberate man and she had not previously noticed his hand shaking. But she said nothing. At supper, she observed how steadily he raised his spoon to his lips and noticed how the tension that had been in his face those last few days had gone. He had been a kind man – a good husband, a good father. But, from that day on, the cat would not go near him, unless it was desperate for food. Even then, it darted in and away from its bowl, never settling, until it was sure it was alone. She hoped he might give thought to why he had done what he had done – where exactly the compulsion lay – but he had never been a reflective man. In turn, she found herself sitting before the fire, trying to reconstruct the journey they had shared. His memories were always lacking in particulars, but she liked to fix incident in her mind – the plucked posy of wildflowers, given early, the way he had bitten on his bottom lip when his son had left and, lately, the boiling water on the cat's back. Her attentiveness to his smallest actions grew, till it felt like prayer. She watched. She waited. It was the time of the evening when he liked to take his silence outside. The sky was rust, the fire low. There was little left in the larder.

### Vocation

He stood at the threshold of the village. He needed time to think. Not many people passed, but when they did, he turned to greet them. Those arriving at the end of that long dusty road assumed he was leaving the village. Those leaving, fearing the prospect of what the road might hold, understood him to be arriving. He found that the roles of welcomer and of encourager satisfied him and the longer he stayed at the threshold of the village, the more it seemed to him that it was for these reasons he had come to be there.

# New Dawn

*John McGlade*

Racing the sun to the horizon, the warning drum:

Get! Up! Get! Up! Get! Up! GET! UP!

Till it's loud enough to crack the world in two; she tumbles out of sleep into her nightmare –

– too late: the feet fall silent; they're here.

Lintel splinters –

– a memory; being scooped from the void; slipping away from marching boots –

– 'Kumba! Kumba!' Her mother's voice brings her back.

'Aye mammy am here!'

But no more words reach her; only shards of sounds half-swallowed by the darkness; she's falling again –

– and groping; but the dark has fingers too. Before she can connect with Kelly or Róisín or Josh or Big D or anybody, her wrist snaps.

The snatched iPhone's glare ignites Home Office livery; stretches across a visor, flies off into the void.

In another world, Kumba can hear her mother crying.

# Extract from the novel
# *William John Jackie for short*

*Nick Brooks*

The only two yellow balloons left were rising up into the heavens over the heads of the grownups and a small black girl was crying, being comforted, pointing up at the sky, the converging tart blueness, the rest of their party on swings, on the roundabout, clambering up a rust-brown slide like soldier ants over some monumental stick insect, a few baggy shorts and kneepads in the skatepark eightsome-reeling up over its concrete cupola and back down again and anyway those teenagers were meant to be in class just now not skiving about here, a big queue of wee ones standing at the ice cream van, all getting treated to a Mr Whippy, the supply teacher trying to keep order, telling everyone to eat their cones quickly, before they melt in the sun. The wee ones were careful to keep away from the duck pond. It was dangerous. A boy had drowned in there only this summer. They were keeping off the grass. They weren't talking to strangers.

It was too hot by far for a hat today, far too hot. William John was breathing much harder, adjusting his sunglasses under the brim of his baseball cap, caught on his own breath, not meaning to be. Bad to let the Chi rise up like that but it had looked as though someone pushed Billy over or knocked off his specs. William John was watching him pick something off the ground from the other side of the climbing-frame. Billy was playing with two other kids, the teacher telling them too late to be careful not to drop anything. The ground was dirty, she was saying far too late and their faces turned up to her, Billy and the other two. A nice teacher, a pleasant round face, a decent face. Mrs Lane must actually be a very good teacher to get their respect like that. Any teacher who could get their respect like that would get William John's respect as well, if it was justified, if they were decent. William John had respected his teachers when he was at school too. If he didn't respect them he got the strap.

The park was so busy today, a Thursday. Always a blessing to have sun in September, the dappled sunshine on all their faces, receiving of the gift, all these children running about, so much screaming and shouting. Billy amongst them, Billy named after himself: William John, Jackie for short.

Billy had been kneeling down for something on the ground, something saltedpink. O, it was a cake. William John could make it out now. A saltpink cake, a fairy cake, Billy must have dropped it, or someone had knocked it from his hands, William John was so close to him, so close. The first time seeing him for months. Billy flicking something from the cake, laughing. Biting into it, pink and white icing sticking around his mouth. His hair was longer now, treacled, curlier. Smiling laughing face, so beautiful, such a beautiful boy, here in the autumn sun, joyous. No one had pushed him, he was all right. It was okay. It was all right.

One of the supply teachers, the classroom assistants, was looking this way. William John walking toward the duck pond, not hurrying, just walking. Taking his time, at his ease, no problem, no trouble. Sodden mulchy ground underfoot even in the sunshine, even now in the sun. He wasn't to stare at his feet. Correcting that, his posture, standing with a straighter spine and the Chi sunk in his belly, in the Dan Tien. Now by the railings looking over at the island in the middle of the pond, where were the ducks though? Flown south already for the winter, no, not yet, there was a mallard, iridescent green feathers around his throat like oil on water. A Scandinavian expression: offering your throat. The lamb offering his throat to the wolf. Christ offering his to Pilate.

The mallard bobbing his head under, bum up in the air. He could feel the man coming up behind him, but William John would deny, deny.

Excuse me, sir, a voice behind him was saying. Clear, undeniable. Sir!

William John began to walk faster, he could hear the man getting closer and he was about to turn. The hand on his elbow, insistent, not forceful, trying to read him. William John pulling away, Don't he was saying. Don't. Without contact the red T shirt couldn't use listening jing. All he'd have left would be Empty Force. William John's hands up in the air. Hands up. Hands up. Marksmen training their laser sights on you. Searching himself for the telltale red spot. Couldn't see it on him. O no, it was on his forehead then. The coming snap that would end him. Hands up, hands up, but his hands were up and surely they could see, surely they could see his hands reach up in supplication and o this was how they had done in John F, with a bullet through the back of the head.

O no, no, not yet. Please.

Billy, Billy his son couldn't see this. O no not this. Not his son.

He was wrenching his hands free and swinging his arms, just swinging them at the red T shirt, blows were landing, the man was backing off and saying something. William John not using closed fists, open palms only, not wanting to put the T shirt down. Just lead him into The Void. Putting him down would land him in court again, no one would listen to him again. Lucky these T shirts had no skill, their listening jing was poor, nonexistent, Void, hurting them couldn't stop JFK's bullet anyway. All the kids were standing there, looking. O not his son, not Billy. His cap came off, it sailed sharply away over the fence into the duck pond and William John was turning away from all the faces trying to read him and jumped over the fence onto the sour grass on the other side. The man in the red tee shirt was just staring at him, shaking his head. He was gesturing to some of the others coming over. William John always respected his teachers but these people weren't worthy of his respect. They were just thugs. They were goons. Informants posing as teachers when the job of a teacher was to help, it was to assist the young. How could they say they were assisting the young when they prevented him from talking to his boy. How could they say they were good people, decent people, if they behaved like this. Preventing him from even seeing his son.

The man was saying he knew William John. He'd warned him before. He was calling the police.

William John kept looking at him, walking along the bank, then stepping into the water. A whipping of wings and a bird of some kind loosing itself into the air. He had disturbed it. Two others had joined the man in the red tee shirt, they all wore red T-shirts, that was no uniform a proper teacher would wear. The three red men were spreading out, going around the perimeter so William John waded backward into the water, up to his thighs. Skin recoiling from the cold, backed in up to his neck.

Okay, the red man was saying. Okay.

Yes?

Okay, okay. Calm down sir.

Yes? Okay?

Okay, okay.

The red men backed off together, watching. William John stopped where he was. They were talking now, glancing at him. He kept still, in the water. The crowds of children were watching them, their games were temporarily suspended, he couldn't see Billy now. Where was Billy in all of this, where was his boy. The men in red were walking away. They were abandoning him and ushering the kids away, over towards the car park, they were cutting their trip short. O he had spoiled their day out for them. O no, no. That wasn't meant to happen at all. He'd never wanted that, they were just kids, why should they be punished. Why should the children suffer. It was unfair, it was wrong.

William John came over to the bank, stepping out of the water, the ducks on that side waggling away from him. The kids were forming a line, the red tee shirts moving them towards the car park, the minivans. One straggler, one last waif on the slide, crying, shouting *Wait!* A wailing voice. *Wait, wait for me!*

Off running after, the last child, and he was alone in the wilderness with the ducks.

# Preface to the novel *Buffalo*

*Jennifer McCartney*

(10.35 Buffalo, NY)

The train is 35 minutes late.

My grandfather had a miniature America in his basement. No cites or flags or iconic urban buildings – only landscape, pipe cleaner trees and the arteries of train tracks across the spray-painted turf. On the wall was the perpetual sun in a pink-sponged sunset. There was a papier-mâché volcano. His Z model train cars included the CN Rail, Pacific Union, Norfolk Southern, engines, cabooses and coal cars.

He made them run – and with no schedule, they were always on time.

I could have flown. Flying is easy, it's cosmopolitan, and it's useful. Flights are quick, airports are clean, cool and the duty free is full of cigarettes and gold jewellery. An

airport however, is a preparation for death – an exercise in fear and faith. I take pills. I drink beer and sleep. At cruising altitude, I resist recording my fears in case my doubtful words have more power than prayer.

The train arrives.

So I have decided this: there is more opportunity for adventure on a train. The rootless and wandering know this. Songwriters know this. Writers know this. Patricia Highsmith had strangers on her train. There was a murder on Agatha Christie's Orient Express and David Baldacci wrote about the California Zephyr at Christmas. From Kerouac's *On the Road* to Edith Nesbit's *The Railway Children* to the obvious Hogwart's Express, the literary world has paid close attention to the romance of the railroad.

I have a ticket and a seat number and someone is sitting in my seat. This is a suitable amount of adventure I suppose.

We begin our journey to New York City, and as an observer to trees and the graffitied backs of buildings I feel that a train traveller is part of something. At least this is what I want to believe. I am a sentimental tourist but am sentimental about little else. I do not marvel at children, brides or puppies. I have a cat and despise items with cat pictures on them. But movement, for me, is moving. A conductor, an engineer, is old America. It is how it used to be and how it was and how it will never be again. A train is an exercise in nostalgia and I am only one of many, perhaps, that find their journeys unique and meaningful and I resist the idea that this makes it all meaningless, this shared enjoyment.

(11.30 Rochester)
A border control guard in sunglasses escorts a Hispanic woman, her two children and their luggage off the train.

(12.00 outside Syracuse.)
A heron in the water.

From Chicago to Utah I once counted twenty-seven bald eagles.

The train continues and always *always* is an awareness of travel, of community and movement and purpose.

Train travel is not purely innocent of course, despite its current environmental advantages. The North American railroad system is a symbol of an empire built on cheap labour – the tracks mapped out and built across plains and blasted through mountains by the unwaged, non-unionised and low-waged.

African American, Irish and Chinese immigrants from east to west lived in shanty towns and died from explosive blasts, scurvy, cave-ins and falling rock – these men integral to the solidification of Canada's sovereignty and America's wealth, yet unwelcome in their cities. As the golden spike was hammered into the ground near Ogden Utah, and the iron spike at Craigellachie BC, so the independence of Canada, and the wealth of America was built upon the backs of the least among us.

*Disappearing Moon Café* by Sky Lee is one of several novels to beautifully narrate the story of the railroad camps in British Columbia.

(4.00 Albany?)
I buy a Snickers and a coffee from the snack bar.

(6.45 Yonkers)
And so, nine hours later we approach Penn station, sliding along the Hudson River in the dusk. I see lights on a bridge, a shopping cart, a blackened car. I see another heron, standing on a rubber tire.

I am a Canadian traveller in a foreign country that looks suspiciously like my own, and I am closer now – to tomorrow, and the next thing.

# Birdie Chorus (after Aristophanes)

*Sally Evans*


fu

fu

epo

me me me me me
jeepers jeepers

epopopopoi

sweary sweary
fuckety fuckety fuck

epopopoi popoi

what a crowd what a crowd what a pong
sun coming sun coming

dammit dammit couldnt sleep

darkdarkdarkdarkdark
murkmurkmurk sunbeam

hopopopoi popoi

live in the trees and be happy
live in the trees is the way

comeoncomeon

swooping swallows back in town
cuckoo cunt back on the brae

trollollolloll ollollol

bickering bluetits
fieldbirds and waterbirds
skybirds and fliers
birds that live in holes on banks
and them that nest on cliffs and rocks
wandering hoopoes trailing twitchers
sweettalkers foulmouths and bitchers

cmon cmon cmon cmon
fuckety fuckety fuck
yell yer heads off
wake up everybirdy
the day is ours

epopo

fu

# The Buntings of the Isle of Mull name themselves

*Seth Crook*

The Corn Bunting (rare, almost extinct).
The Ortolan Bunting (extremely scarce,
one adult female seen on a campsite in 2009).

The Reed Bunting (scarce resident breeding species,
breeds in reed beds, or reads in bed, records patchy).
The Brambling (uncommon, not really a Bunting.
Often seen rambling without a 'B').

The Snow Bunting (winter visitor, tiny numbers).
The Scarce Bunting (very common).
The Absent Bunting (always here).

The Hang Out More Bunting (appears on special occasions only).
The Extinct Bunting (numbers booming).
The Amazingly Graceful Bunting (was lost but now is found
was blind but now can see).

# Small thoughts

*Seth Crook*


of cups of tea
and the next trolley round.
Of her, back in the garden.
I'd like to hear the buzz of bees.

I try to read,
but not caring enough about the great vote,
I let the paper fall,
covering my eyes. Nose in page 7.

The Mulleach in the next bed
fiddles with his radio,
until he finds the tunes of the 1970s.
I understand. He has what I have.


# The April Birds Proclaim their Natural Rights

*Seth Crook*


By right of swoop,
the buzzard rules the heather.
By coconutty right,
the gorse can take a kiss.
All sounds will bee
by right of hidden cuckoo. Listen.
We'll reign, all Spring,
by higher right of bliss. Know this.

# Naidheachd / News-Gizzen / News

*Maggie Rabatski, Sheila Templeton, A C Clarke*

### Naidheachd

Saoil dè naidheachd
a bheirinn thugad
air an àit'.

An innsinn dhut
gu bheil gàrradh grànnd'
an-diugh ris a' chladach,
ged nach eil sìon a' fàs
san lios a bhuannaich thu
bho sgeinean na gaoith'.

An innsinn
gu bheil am fonn
far na thog thu
na sgaothan bhuntata
cruaidh fo chùirtearan feòir,
is an cuan glas a sìor bhualadh
gun chuimhn' ort,
gun chuimhn' ort.

An innsinn mar a dh'fhàg mi
ro chiaradh na h-oidhch',
air eagal bho shùilean aognaidh
uinneagan gun sholas.

'S e b'fhearr leam innse
gu bheil caoraich fhathast air na raoin,
is an cìobair càirdeach dhuinn fhèin;
gu bheil altachadh fhathast roimh bhiadh
an taigh mhic do bhràthar,
's nuair a chrom sinn ar cìnn,
bha do ghuth sèimh fhèin
ri ar taobh.

**News-Gizzen**

Fit news
wid I fesh ye
o this place i noo?

I cud spik aboot
i coorse watter-brak
spleet-new alang i strand,
an spik mair aboot fit wye
naething growes in i gairden
ye warsled fae snell oot-wins.

I cud nyatter on
aboot i bonnie grun far ye graiped up
pearly buds o new tatties
aa saddit noo in lang wiry girse;
fyle i grizzelt sea tyauves on
aathing foryat, aathing foryat.

I cud tell ye
that I took flicht afore mirkin
feart for i chilpie glower
o dairkened windaes.

But I'd raither tell ye
how yowes breenge still ower green parks
an i chiel wi i sma black tyke
has oor name;
that bethankit still cams afore meal an maut
in i hoose o yer brither's loon;
an fan we closed wir een for i gweed-words
it wis your vyce in that room.

## News

What could I tell you now of the places
you never made your own, which once
spoke of you, as a bottle which held spirit
speaks of its absence. I could say
that the house you lived in thirty years
is penned by scaffolding, the pergola
you burdened with roses waits for burial,

that five tower blocks stamp on the grounds
of the grand house you pretended was ours,
its shrubberies and tennis court
greened over by municipal turf,
no ball games allowed. I could say
your ashes have been scattered over coffins
whose headstone wears a wreath of names

not one of them yours. I hope I would tell you
how the books you bought me, their battered covers
an unfailing promise, live in my mind,
how your pottery hedgepig sits on the shelf
which guards their multiplied descendants
and when I kissed your cold forehead
it was I who asked forgiveness.

# Fr Meslier* in his study / Maighstir Meslier na Sheomar-leughaidh / Faither Meslier Amang His Buiks

*A C Clarke, Maggie Rabatski, Sheila Templeton*

**Fr Meslier* in his study**

I love to hear the clop of cows
to the milking shed, their snorted breath
a whiter vapour than the mist
distilling off chilled pastures.
I love how they inhabit space
the bulk of their shoulders.

The world is stirring with the sun.
The fields have rhythms, need no bells.
A cock crows in a yard near by.
A woman's out feeling for eggs
under the hens' warm feathers.
Steady, the cows move down the lane.

Water nests in the ewer, night-staled.
I pour some in the basin, wash
then take my stole, bind the sad stare
of the crucifix. Ah, Son of Man,
I might have fought to save you if
you had stayed carpenter.

*Jean Meslier, C18 French priest who secretly professed atheism.

## Maighstir Meslier na Sheomar-leughaidh

Is caomh leam fuaim a' chruidh-bhainne
air ghluasad gu bleoghann na maidne,
anail an cuinnlean nas gile
nan fhuar-cheo tha 'g èirigh far a' bhuaile.
Is toil leam cho daingeann 's tha'n giùlan,
meud mhòr an guailnean.


Tha'm baile tighinn beo ris a' ghrèin,
chaneil feum air glag ach a-mhàin
 caismeachd an fhearainn fhèin
coileach a' gairm san iodhlainn ud thall,
làmh nìghne sireadh ugh
fo itean bhlàth nan cearc.
Socair, an crodh a' gabhail seachad.


Tha'm bùrn air fàs searbh
san t-soitheach oidhch';
siud steall dhan mhias gus m'ionnlaid,
suainidh mi an uair sin mo stoc
mu shuilean tùrsach a' chrois-sgiùrsaidh.
O Mhic an Duine, is mathaid
gu robh mi air strì gus do theàrnadh
nam biodh tu air leantainn nad shaor.

**Faither Meslier Amang His Buiks**

Ma hairt lifts at the skreek o day
faan I hear the kye plowterin past,
big shooders warslin for space
in ma windae, udders swingin ticht
desperate tae let doon their milk,
breath smokin white lik the pearly haar
jist lichtnin ower the ley-girse.

The hale warld is pirlin wi the sun.
Parks lilt tae their ain sang, nae need for bells.
A cockieleerie blaws news o this morn.
The kitchie-deem's oot bye, feelin for eggs
unnerneath waarm chucken fedders.
And the kye pace, quate-lik doon the loan.

Watter fae last nicht lies foostit in its joug.
I pour some intae the bowlie, gie ma face
a quick cat's dicht, tak ma shawl,
afore I daur the doolsome glower
o the crucifix. Ach, Son o Man
I wad hae been yer bonnie fechter
had ye been content tae bide a jyner.

# Lairnin Aboot Luve / Leasan / Lesson in Love

*Sheila Templeton, Maggie Rabatski, A C Clarke*

**Lairnin Aboot Luve**

He cairriet Paddy tae the car,
the auld blue-bottle Morris.

They didnae cam hame til aifterneen,
the usual time for thir entry, garten
wi danglin leggy hare or rubbit.

It wis still winter-time, but a saft day.
So a grave cud be dug as easy as that
can iver be, fan the tall chiel, my granda
cam roun the side o the hoose, cradlin
a sma black tyke, swaddled in a saick.

Naebody helped. An naebody hinnered.
Even we bairnies didnae ask.

Grunnie wis baking, fillin the kitchen
wi a mound o gowden bannocks.

He sat ootside tae clean his gun;
then washed himsel at the kitchen sink,
forsakin oor new bathroom upstairs.

I lairnit aboot luve that day.
He wid niver have used sic a word.

**Leasan**

Ghiùlain e Dìleas na ghàirdean
a- mach gu ruig' a' chàir,
an t-seann Mhorris dhorcha-gorm.

Chan fhacas a-rithist iad gu feasgar,
an t-am bu ghnàthach dhaibh tilleadh,
geàrr neo coineanach an crochadh nan cois.

'S gann a bha 'n geamhradh seachad
ach bha taisead san aimsir,
deagh là, ma tha leithid ann
airson uaigh a chladhach –
nuair a nochd e, mo sheanair àrd socair,
timcheall ceann an taighe,
cù beag dubh suaint' a-nis
ann am poca.

Bha granaidh a' fuine,
a' lìonadh a' chidsin
le sgonaichean òrach.

Shuidh esan a-muigh
a' glanadh a ghunna.
Cha deach duine na chòir ga chuideachadh,
cha deach duine na chòir,
cha chualas fiù 's ceist bhuainne a' chlann.

Nigh e a làmhan aig an t-sinc
ged bha 'n seòmar-ionnlaid ùr
shuas an staidhre.

Fhuair mise leasan 'sa ghaol an là ud,
ged nach toireadh esan an t-ainm sin air.

### Lesson in Love

You carried the cat you'd raised from a kitten
in the old wicker basket,
came back from the vet in an hour
basket dangling
from your gardener's hand.

It was still winter-time but a gentle day
the kind when it's easy to imagine
the sky holding its anger back,
wrapping a grey street in its soft shroud.

You walked through the door, no change
in your face that I could see.
You said nothing.

I was cooking supper, filling the kitchen
with the comfort of soup.

You sat in the living-room, without music,
books or even a pencil, just sat.
Much later you told me you'd cried

silently all the way home. It was love.
Not that you'd ever have said.

# The Cryptographer's Song

*Andy Jackson*

It takes time to generate these ciphers;
the symbols on the shopping lists,
the codewords on the national news,
the knowing randomness of crossword clues
in broadsheets, patterns that we know.
We come and go, leave moments
for each other like a dead letter drop.
Lights go on and off and on in morse.

In Nissen huts the women go to work
assimilating data, raking through the numbers,
in search of sequences or correlations,
knowing nothing is as random as it seems,
that tiny revelations are not accidents of sound
or light. In time they may decrypt the words
we are afraid to say: that both of us would
rather die alone before revealing anything.

# What were you going to do with those 15 minutes?

*Ewan Gault*

Soon enough your headlights reflect off something bright like the eyes of a deer driven by the snow to forage by the roadside or the shattered windows of a smashed-up car. The road twists and turns and has tossed many teenage drivers from its back. Their names appear amongst the wedding photos and court reports in the local paper that your mother posts you every week. Shiver despite the warmth of your car and the glow of your speed dial and fuel gauge. Although you haven't driven on it for years, you know how this road rolls. It is not the road that you're frightened of.

For a moment the trees slip away revealing the loch. A loan boat ferrying timber from the forests of Argyll moves steadily south. You wonder if the men on board are warm, if they are listening to Christmas tunes, if they have places they'd rather be.

'It's so beautiful,' she says, 'so natural.'

You concentrate on the cats' eyes and don't comment on the regimented lines of Corsican pine on the hillside or the nuclear submarines moving freely in the fished-to-extinction-sea. As the beams of your headlights sweep across an inlet they illuminate dense cages in which monster salmon thrash and splash as if they're going places other than the seafood restaurants of Southern England.

You consider telling her about an article in the local paper about salmon that had escaped from one of these fish farms. Even after a lifetime in captivity some migratory instinct had made them search for a place to spawn, but having no home they had grown confused, exhausted, lost, and beached themselves in shallow streams and backwaters.

'How do you feel?' She asks

'Euphoric,' you say.

She holds onto the door as you negotiate a couple of bends, the car drifting a little: the first suggestion of ice.

'Euphoric?'

'Euphoric,' you reply, letting the word flail and crack like a frayed rope whip.

She hugs herself like a person exposed to the all surrounding cold, who realises that their own body is the only source of warmth.

The road lurches down the peninsula, and a village's Christmas tree, decorated only above the reach of delinquent teens, flashes against the dark. The pub that first served you drink is here and you slow as much to gawk at the shivering souls sucking on their cigarettes as to observe the reduced speed limit. You feel reassured that the same ravaged faces have not left their posts. Haloed by smoke, illuminated by street lights, robed in never-in-fashion clothes, they peer into the darkness as if fearing that the Vikings, who their ancestors guarded this coastline against, might materialise on the loch's shore.

Like never ageing sentinels carved in rock you think, before recognising a woman who looks like a half melted wax work of a girl you once fancied in school. The others: withered, balding and bloated were at your school as well. You try to remember if there was something that might have damned them to a life spent hanging around this village whose utility vans and cenotaph bear all of their names.

In the rear view mirror you notice a car, probably captained by some boy-racer, rapidly gaining ground on you. Even though it is stupid, even though you are half an hour from the end of a nine hour journey, you accelerate round the bend and remember doing this during the last months of school before leaving this place for university, for jobs, for her, for good.

Thirty minutes until the homecoming, the parents smaller and more hesitant than you remembered them. There will be that smell: pine wood and fish soup. And it'll seem so potent and familiar at first but by the second day you won't notice it at all. On the walls there will be decorations brought out of an ancient cardboard box: circuit broken fairy lights, tinsel that has lost its sparkle, hopelessly tangled and tatty but never thrown out.

'We need to get our story right.'

'Our,' she cracks the window open as if releasing a bad smell, 'story.' The temperature in the car drops and you reach to turn up the heating, but before you've twisted the dial she has closed the window. 'Well, if you're sure, if we're sure that we're doing the right thing.'

The inside of the car is illuminated and you look in the mirror as the full beam of the following car is flashed, on and off.

'Idiot,' you mutter, but again increase the pressure on the accelerator remembering the disdain you felt, aged 17, when stuck behind some day-tripper, who cautiously negotiated these roads, when all you wanted was to veer round corners, feeling your heart thump, tasting the contents of your stomach, knowing you were alive.

'What?'

'Not you, him.'

'I just can't go on like this any longer.'

Concentrate on the road, on the lane markers, on ensuring that the kid in the chasing vehicle is not shouting insults about the car in front that is so much more powerful than his but is being driven by someone who shouldn't even be on the road at this time at night.

'I thought we'd decided.'

'Well we had, but it's not a certainty until anyone else knows.'

The car behind is now tail-gating you. Its headlights are on full-beam and despite the fact that you are swinging the car round corners you can't shake him. On a blind bend he overtakes you, and even though you knew it was coming, the ferocity of his accelerating engine, the rock-salt being thrown from the road by his tyres, still shocks you.

'What's he thinking? It's twenty miles to the end of the road. There's no ferry anymore.

The pubs won't be closed for a couple of hours. I mean how much time is he going to save anyway?'

'Fifteen minutes.'

'Fifteen minutes? If that. And what can you do with fifteen minutes?'

She sighs as a way of saying that if she needs to answer this question, then you really are a lost cause.

The road has switched from the east of the peninsula to the west and in the moonlight you catch the outline of Jura.

'Skye,' she says.

–

'Islay?'

'Closer.'

She kneads her head and you know that she will be going over the labels of the whisky bottles that you keep prominently displayed in your Bethnal Green flat.

'Jura,' she says triumphantly.

'And the closer one is Gigha and soon, if the moon stays out, we'll see Islay.' The home straight you had always thought when returning from university in Glasgow.

'Have you any water?'

Water, you think, it is everywhere: cascading from the hills; darkly rippling in sea-lochs that claw at the boggy land; and spread out before you in an ocean that stretches all the way to Canada. Argyll has more coastline than France, you think about saying, but, knowing that you've told her this a dozen times, instead pass her a plastic bottle half-full of car warmed water that has travelled the nine hours from London. She glugs it down, this liquid that has been through seven human bodies and which clogs up shower-heads, makes her hair dry and fluffy and scales the inside of your kettle with eczema like flakes.

'Listen. We're going to be there soon. If we're telling them, we need to be certain.'

You know that after arriving you will ask your parents for some water and they will present it in a pint glass that has your name inscribed on the side. This is the same pint glass that they gave to you on your 18th birthday to mark the start of adulthood, your first steps out into the wide world. You will wonder why you never took that pint glass with you. The water will be icy cold and because you haven't drank anything since passing Manchester you will gulp it down and let out a satisfied sigh. Relieved, your mother will start with news from the town: births, deaths, marriages, all involving people you can barely recall. Slowly but surely the conversation will trail back down the road: questions about whether you noticed the new school in Lochgilphead or that three shops in Inveraray had changed owners or how you found the motorway extension in Glasgow.

To break the silence you will hand back the pint glass and say, 'Now that's real water. You don't get water like that down South.'

Yes, there may be no jobs for you, but the water tastes nice. Go, gorge yourself on it.

'There's something I have to say, something I've been meaning to say but, are you even listening?'

You stamp on the brake and clutch pedals; tyres shriek like an eagle whose nest is being raided and you grip onto the steering wheel as your body snaps into the strap's tight grip. On the road at a weird angle is the car that overtook you. Unclip the seatbelt and open your door, exhaling a ghostly apparition that drifts away from your headlights. The engine of the other vehicle is still ticking and an aria plays softly from inside. On the bonnet you see the back end of a deer that has smashed through the windscreen. There are no passengers in the car. Taking out your mobile you use the torch function to look at the driver's mashed face, skull caved in from the impact of hitting a 200 kilo red deer.

You only look for a second before calling the emergency services. Although convinced that the driver is dead, you tell the operator that you can't be sure; you want the police and air ambulance to arrive quickly, to take this mess off your hands. Return to your own car and get back in. She is rubbing her belly and squeezing her eyes shut.

'Are you alright?'

–

'What's wrong?'

'I was trying to tell you something.'

'He hit a deer, the other driver. If he hadn't been driving so fast, it could have been us. What was he doing driving like that?'

'Was he playing operatic music?'

'What?'

'Was he playing operatic music?'

You want to open her eyes, to tell her to stop massaging her belly as if she is the one who is hurt. 'Why would you think that?'

'I heard a woman singing when you opened your door and for a moment I wasn't sure where the song was coming from. I couldn't hear it when you got back in. I wanted to be sure.'

You turn on the emergency lights, get out of the car and go stand on the grassy verge. The flashing lights give a festive appearance to proceedings, but turning around you feel the all-encompassing darkness of the sky and the land and the ocean envelope you. Here there is a volume of silence and a dazzling blackness that terrifies an urbanite like you. The thought flits through your mind that darkness is the reality of things, that even great London with its millions of lights is no greater to the universe than a deer's eyes caught in a car's headlights.

'Get out of the car,' you shout, but she has rested her forehead on the dashboard.

You think about going to the car and pulling her out, but instead walk towards the dead man. The radio in his car is talking about road works on the M25 and the Christmas number 1. Tomorrow is going to be fine. Cold but fine, the weather forecaster tells a man who will never feel the sun on his face again. You play the light from your mobile across the mess of antler and skull, blood and bone.

A mobile rings from within the car. You open the driver's door and lift the phone from the man's jacket pocket. He is still warm, and there is something sticky on your knuckles.

'Hello.'

'Jim, love, is that you, is that you?' A Northern English voice, shrill with worry. 'I've called you a hundred times.'

'This isn't Jim.'

'But it's Jim's number.'

'Yes, but this isn't Jim'

'Who is this? What's going on?'

You pause, breathe in. Your lungs have never felt so full of air.

'There's been a traffic accident. Jim is dead. I'm sorry. Are you his wife?'

A sound like bathwater disappearing down a plug.

'Where are you? Where is he?'

'We're on the A83.'

—

'The road that goes down the Kintyre Peninsula.'

'The Kintyre Peninsula?'

'Yes.'

'In Scotland?'

'Yes.'

'But Jim phoned me from work this afternoon. He was going to do some Christmas shopping and come home. He lives and works in Liverpool. He's never been to Scotland in his life. He doesn't know anyone in Scotland. This must be some kind of mistake.'

'We're definitely in Scotland.'

'But Jim, are you sure it's him?'

'Well, I've never met him before.'

'Tell me what he looks like.'

'Does he drive a blue polo, registration plate G130 TRK? Does he wear a black leather jacket?'

'Yes, but his face.'

—

'Christ.'

Watch a police car speed along the road. Soon this will all be over.

'How did it happen?'

'He overtook us a few miles back; he was driving like a maniac.'

'To get home?'

'No. In the opposite direction. The road ends in 20 miles. I don't know what would make a man drive like that.'

'He said he was coming home. He said he was coming home.'

The woman starts wailing. As the police car comes to a halt you slip the phone back into the driver's pocket. It starts ringing almost immediately, but you're not going to answer it again.

Two policemen get out. You can hear their feet crunch the rock salt into the roads surface. Both of them were in your school and you wonder what it was about them that made it so obvious they would become policemen.

'Wow,' one of them says looking at the wreck.

'Many inside?'

'Just the one.'

'Dead?'

'Very.'

'Local?'

'I don't think so.'

One of the policemen approaches you. He takes out a notepad, and actually licks the tip of his pencil.

Mumbling the story, you wonder why you feel like you're lying. The policeman nods every so often, but doesn't write anything down.

'And your wife, is she injured?'

'My wife?'

'Your passenger.'

'No, I mean yes, I mean, I don't know.'

The policeman peers at you. 'Sir, you should get her out of the car.'

You remember the policeman's surname is Littlejohn, that he was a good swimmer despite being the wrong shape. You want to ask if he still competes, but instead walk back to your car. Now that the police are here with their cooking gas blue lights and torches and radios and calm uniformed efficiency you feel empty. Only minutes ago you were delivering words heavy as bombs. Now you are precariously light. Open the door. She looks up like she has never seen you before, her eyelids pink and puffy.

A dull throbbing churns the night air. You both look out as a white light bigger than all the other stars makes itself significant.

'An angel,' she says and smiles shyly. 'I was trying to tell you something.'

'I know. I *know*.'

The light looms large in the night sky.

'Are you ok?'

'I'm ok. We're ok.'

You smile, unsure if she was including you.

The light hovers celestially bright and a down blast as if from beating wings whips the hair around your head. The policemen are looking up and Littlejohn is saying words into a radio. Climb into the car and close the door. You are there with her smell and your smell mingling in the vehicle. For a moment a blinding brilliance searches the inside of the car. She reaches out, takes your hand and places it on the curve of her belly. Your hand cradles her warmth. This is home now. Welcome.

# The Scattering

*Diana Hendry*

I was glad of Simon's funeral. Not that he was dead, of course, I wasn't glad about that – though on reflection, I was rather. Simon's been dying for months, each month getting a little more skeletal until you wondered how he could still stand up. Well, towards the end, he couldn't. He was in a wheelchair when I last saw him. It was in the theatre bar after a performance of *One for the Road,* Alan Munford's new play – Alan being an old pal of Simon's – and he had to be brought up in the lift and then somehow helped out of his wheelchair and propped up in an ordinary chair. He wasn't going to be confined. I suppose that's what that was about although it seemed hardly worth the effort because he'd chosen a rather deep armchair so that at home-time it took three people to help him out of it.

I have to say that about the head and face he was looking more and more like a memento mori – gaunt, eyes sunk in their sockets, skin like paper. Simon was one of those who take a long time dying. I've known others. There seems to be no rhyme or reason about it. Why it's sudden and quick for some and long and slow for others. Anyway, it's uncomfortable to watch the long slow ones even when they're brave – as Simon was – possibly that makes it worse. For the rest of us I mean. I found myself thinking that public dying should be forbidden, though you could make an exception for Simon because even though he was 86 and looked like a cadaver, he was still astonishingly handsome. You could see the Simon he had been in his bones. A part of it was his clothes, of course. He was always a dresser, a cashmere and soft cords man; elegant, just on the edge of but not tipping over into, effete. Perhaps his pipe added a saving macho touch.

Sitting in the crematorium chapel along side Stella and Leonard I thought that the only thing I'd really liked about Simon – apart from the fact that he seemed to like me and always touched my arm affectionately when we met – was his handsomeness. Of course he had a voice that went with it. In my opinion it doesn't matter how handsome a man is if his voice is unpleasant. It doesn't work the other way though – or not for me – a man with a lovely voice can get away with being almost ugly.

Anyway, sitting there while various eulogies were read by those who had known Simon as a friend or worked with him the theatre, or gone fishing with him – I felt slightly guilty – fraudulent even – that my affection for Simon was based on such a superficial thing as his looks and, too, that I was so vulnerable to beauty – I've been avoiding the word, but yes, Simon was beautiful – that this won him a fixed place in my affections. I'm not even sure if 'affection' is the right term. I merely liked *looking* at Simon. There was no desire attached it. No curiosity. If I should say to Simon *I'm very pleased to see you,* that summed it up. I felt more affection for him now that he was dead than I had when he was alive. Maybe not affection. Gratitude. Gratitude for dying when he did, just before Christmas so that the funeral had to wait until after, which I know is hard for the family but in my case was just what I wanted. If someone had asked me, round about December 29th, in that period between Christmas and New Year, *what would you like to do today* – the honest answer would have been *I'd like to go to a funeral.*

In part, a funeral seemed just the right antidote to Christmas and prelude to New Year. So much so that I can't think why someone hasn't made it part of winter's ritual, a proper solstice. New Year's Eve is all partying. There's really not enough mourning attached to it. Old Lang Syne doesn't do it for me. Apart from the almost trivial fact that apparently I was in the mood for a funeral, there was something else. In recent months I've become aware of an inexplicable sadness that seemed to have taken root deep down in me like the solid, muddy deposit in the very depths of the pond. Unlodgeable sorrow. I was not unhappy. Mostly I was cheerful, contented even, but all these genuinely good feelings lay on top of the sorrow. As though sorrow/sadness was the true core, as perhaps it is. I've heard it said we carry our own death within us.

It was very peaceful at the crematorium. Had Simon asked for this particular one I wondered? Very likely. Built by a famous architect, it's was shaped like a squeeze box, folds of stone with tall glazed slits for windows and set in parkland with a river running along one side. Non-denominational, it was discreet in its symbols rather proudly allowing for funerals of Christians, Budhist, Hindi, San, Sikh and Tao. There was even a 'Scattering Point' on the river for Sikhs and Taos. Inside was dark and calm with long pine pews and a platform of white concrete and bronze where the coffin rested. Simon wasn't anything, though one of his eulogists referred to a Jewish great grandfather who'd travelled from Lithuania and how Simon, this friend felt, would have wished to acknowledge this. It was the only faith not mentioned by the crematorium.

There were no prayers and no singing but I didn't mind. It had come upon me suddenly, the realisation that I wasn't there for Simon. I was there for my dead lover, Mark and my dead mother-in-law Jessica. I was at Simon's funeral because I hadn't been at theirs. And not being at theirs had left me feeling what? Uncomfortable. As if I was still carrying them around with me.

Why hadn't I gone to Mark's funeral? It would have been a Quaker one. Various friends, members of the family, would have spoken. Said nice things. Said loving things. I could have spoken. I could have said how his imagination had always half amused, half enchanted me. Enchanted. Yes. I'd been enchanted. What would have been the upset in that? The fear of upsetting had kept me away. I'd not wanted to upset Mark's daughters who knew of my existance, or his wife who with more than generosity tolerated my existance, my place in Mark's affections. At least this was the reason I gave myself, though in retrospect I became aware – was it the obituary notice that spoke of his wife as *his beloved Eileen* – as my place as also-ran, minor part, second fiddle et cetera in Mark's life.

At least I'd managed, on the day of his funeral, to go off to a quiet place among the tall, dark pines in the Botanic Gardens, to think about him. Which is more than I'd managed to do for Jessica. I became aware of just how much Jessica had been on my conscience about halfway through the service for Simon. A rather nervous and clearly amateur violinist was struggling through a Bach suite when it occurred to me that possibly I was using Simon as a kind of surrogate for Jessica.

Perhaps it was the knowledge of the Scattering Point on the river that prompted me to remember Jessica's ashes being taken home to Scotland as she'd always wished. I'd badly wanted to be there although 'badly' is perhaps the right word. *Badly* because I knew my being there would have angered Angus, my ex, and *badly* because I was enjoying a pleasant fantasy about turning up at the cemetry where Jessica was to be scattered among her ancestors, as the mysterious Other Woman, silent but of course darkly beautiful. (A hat or some head covering seemed very important to this fantasy). Did I love Jessica? Did I want to be there beause I loved her? Not exactly. Fond. Yes. And admiring, although my admiration was for her glamour (c.f. Simon), her lovers, her independence and her dedication to her profession as a physiotherapist. She'd been the first independent, working woman I'd ever known.

Angus hated her. Never forgave her for abandoning him to the grandparents and a housekeeper while she was off trying to earn a living and, as a divorced woman, perhaps seeking a new man. She was, it must be admitted, incredibly manipulative and/or charming, depending on your response, but if the former, how long can a son remain unforgiving of his mother? Unto death it would seem. And as Angus was also unforgiving of me, Jessica and I had this unforgivingness in common. Long after my own divorce, Jessica and I stayed friends so that I was prone to joke that you can divorce a man but not a mother-in-law.

According to my daughter, the continued relationship, (full of Angus gossip and shared complaint), was 'inappropriate'. *Inappropriate* is a key word in Debbie's vocabulary. A counselling word, I suspect. Instead of an action or deed being good, bad or indifferent, loving, cruel or unkind, the moral judgement rested on the deed's appropriateness.

Anyway, I thought it was just Debbie's youth that me her think a continued relationship with an ex mother-in-law known for sixteen years, was inappropriate. Nevertheless, it was for Debbie's sake that I decided not to go to witness the scattering of Jessica's ashes. Debbie has sufferend enough of the tug of love between mother and father. Her loyalties would be horribly torn if we were both there. So I'd told Jessica's daughter (another continued relationship) that on the day of the scattering I'd go to the Catholic Cathedral and light a candle for her mother. For Jessica. The Catholic Cathedral because – and again to Angus's annoyance – without exactly turning Catholic, Jessica was drawn that way. Had a knack of befriending nuns.

It was pouring with rain and blowing a gale on the day of the Scattering. The Catholic Cathedral turned out to be much further away than I'd thought. Something else cropped up. I couldn't be bothered. What was one candle, etc etc? Reason after poor reason. Though I did do it, several weeks later and in the Anglican Cathedral (decaff Christianity as I recall Simon calling it) but it didn't feel quite right. Out of sync. Not part of the ritual. It felt as if I'd failed her.

The violinist finished playing Bach. I observed a woman at the front – daughter, sister, mistress? – wiping her eyes. It is always better for everyone if someone cries. Observing her made me think that considering onself, querying love and/or worrying about upsetting others, was entirely beside the point. When it comes to funerals, the question to ask oneself, wasn't to do with love or upset or inappropriateness, it was *does this person – did Mark, did Jessica – want me to be there?* And the answer in both cases was yes. It came to me that Jessica would have liked me to be at the Scattering out of pure mischief; to upset folk (particularly Angus) and to create a little drama. Bagpipes, me and a little drama. That's what Jessica would have liked.

Before Simon was whooshed away, we were all asked to lay a flower on his rather fine wooden coffin. There was a basket full of chrsyanthumum heads. I chose two white ones.

Did Simon want me to be there, I wondered?

Probably not.

# A Song Died

*Andrew McLinden*

Look around this vegetarian café; see the women sitting at round tables, eating square cakes, talking about love triangles. Most of them are thirty plus. One or two are nudging fifty. Your sister was diagnosed when she was twenty four.

You write the word *diagnosed* down on your notepad and see that it's an anagram of *a song died*. You've had a thing about anagrams most of your life. They often reveal hidden truths. Your personal favourite is *Arnold Schwarzenegger* which makes: *he's grown large n crazed*.

The waitress comes over and you order tea for yourself and coffee for your sister. You also order her a side of Madeira cake because this was/is her favourite. You still go through this ritual every Saturday afternoon. Even though she's dead, even though she's not going to eat the cake or drink the coffee. The waitress gets it. She doesn't charge you. She keeps it in its wrapper and then places it back on the display after you've gone. The waitress went to school with your sister, used to compliment her every Saturday on her head scarves.

You sip at the tea and it tastes sweet. You place the cup back down on the saucer and think about it. Then you sip at it again. Sugar has never bothered you before but you imagine its corrosive qualities as it lays siege to your teeth. 'Sugar,' you say, to the lady on your left.

She rolls her eyes and her friends start laughing as she folds the napkin down on the table. 'Don't call me sugar,' she says.

So you are in bed with your wife and it is getting on for seven years of sex. In the blackness of the room you are just two genderless shapes grunting and you've tried everything to get it going again. You've tried making love. You've tried role play. You've tried shouting out the names of each other's friends. This led to her hiding behind the Cornflakes box at breakfast next morning; she placed that yellow-beaked cockerel in the middle of the table like a cardboard partition.

This night you are trying to imagine she is someone else: Kylie Minogue, Scarlett Johansson, Sandra from the office. But they don't get you going either. So your wife, and Scarlett, and Kylie, and Sandra, they all climb off and all five of you lie like that side by side panting on the bed, staring up at the ceiling.

She says, 'What's wrong now?'

And you tell her that she should have an affair, that she should just take someone else for that side of things. You tell her you wouldn't mind – that we all have needs. The shock of this statement sucks the air out of the room. It is the most shocking thing ever said between you, right up until she says, 'I'm already having an affair.' Then someone starts crying there in the darkness. Could be you could be her could be the Hollywood actress. And the more this voice unburdens itself the more you think of sugarless tea and how you made the right decision to quit. Next night at work you're playing with anagrams. From *eleven plus two,* you get: *twelve plus one.* From *a decimal point,* you get: *I'm a dot in place.*

At your break, you feel inside your pocket for your cigarettes and then stop because you realise that *a carton of cigarettes = I got a taste for cancer.* You crush the packet and throw it in the bin. You take a deep breath and pop a mint, then go back inside.

At the booth you buy an extra train ticket for your sister and come home on the eight forty from Queen Street. You sit there as the train goes in and out of tunnels, listening to the woman behind you as she talks to her friend. She says that someone called Archie is at death's door. You turn round and stare at her.

'What does death's door look like?' you ask her.

The lady and her friend exchange glances.

'Does it have a welcome mat? Does it have a brass knocker? How would you describe it?'

'It's not something I think about,' she says. 'It's just a saying.'

'Ah,' you say nodding, 'Death's door is actually a trap door. One minute you're walking along the street texting and the next minute you're hurtling through the darkness of space. Was it a car or a coronary? Who can say?'

About a hundred yards from the house where you live, you see your wife in a man's car. You stop and stare. They are kissing. When they've finished kissing your wife gets out and pats down her dress. Then she waves him off, and you can see by the way she's standing – toes folded and heels off the ground – that she's still reaching for him even as the distance increases. And even though you encouraged it in a way, even though you shouldn't be bothered, you are terribly bothered.

In the Admiral you sit down beside Saint Michael. He is called this because every week he turns wages into wine. You like Saint Michael because he laughs at your jokes. It is very important to have a friend like this. You finish the last of your beer and place the empty glass down on the table.

'Want another one?' Saint Michael asks.

'No,' you reply, 'I'm giving up.'

And he starts laughing, even though you haven't told a joke.

Back in the house your eyes settle on the television. She's watching a movie. You turn *The Titanic Disaster* into: *Death; it starts in ice.*

Adverts are the only time of the day when you feel someone is genuinely interested in you. So you watch them till the end. Then you unplug the television set and lift if off the stand. She opens the door to let you out but she's biting her bottom lip. 'You know how it ends anyway,' you say. You step out onto the patio and drop it to the ground. The television explodes and all the life and drama that was once housed within it is released. The ghosts of TV shows past and present are exorcised as the glass shatters: jet fighters shoot out into the night sky pursued by space ships. Ghosts and ghouls wrestle with each other as they fall into the hedges. Never ending rounds of canned laughter are released and they echo off the walls and windows of your housing estate before heading skywards, as newscasters, presidents, and gardening show hosts chatter their way towards oblivion. After it's over the television set sits there injured like a dumb animal, with circuit boards that no longer connect and buttons that no longer press with purpose.

You walk in and close over the door. You wipe your feet on the mat. You watch your wife as she runs the iron over a shirt. You see how unhappy you've made her. You decide she'd be better off with her boyfriend. They can have sex that ends in climaxes rather than recriminations. Somewhere between the cuff and collar, sleeve says leave. At first it is awkward.

'But I don't want to go,' she says.

'Go live with your boyfriend,' you tell her.

'I don't know if he's ready for that.' As she says this her eyes well and she brings her hand to her mouth. 'You need to let go of your sister.' She rests the iron upright and takes a deep breath. 'You can't just spring something like this on me out of the blue. We need to talk.'

'We need to talk,' says your boss.

'It's the elephant in the room,' says the woman from HR.

'We've tried everything we can think of,' says your boss.

'We need to get our ducks in a row,' says the woman from HR.

'If you leave without going to the union we can still give you a reference.'

'No need to shoot the puppy.'

'It's company policy that I escort you from the premises.'

'Let's deal with the crocodile closest to the canoe.'

In the kitchen you open up the cupboards and look at all the ingredients and instructions but it is too complicated and you decide that you'd be as well giving up on food as well.

Three days you lie in bed waiting. You move onto longer anagrams. *To be or not to be: that is the question, whether it's nobler in the mind to suffer the slings and arrows of outrageous fortune,* turns into: *In one of the Bard's best thought of tragedies, our insistent hero, Hamlet, queries on two fronts about how life turns rotten.* This one delights you. Next you try this: *That's one small step for a man, one giant leap from mankind.* You get: *a thin man ran; makes a large stride, left planet, pins flag on moon! On to Mars!*

You force yourself up onto your feet to take your own giant leap and examine yourself in the mirror. Your beard is coming in thick and black. It suits you. You rub at it while ruminating on an idea. This idea being that how you give up says a lot about your character.

Exhibitionists

*ex*hibition*ist*s

exhibi*ti*onists

*ex*hibi*ti*onists

They jump off tall buildings with crowds watching below – showmen to the last. Nihilists crave annihilation and give head to the double barrel of a shotgun. Pessimists choke down pills with strong liquor and then lie back on a sofa, with framed photos of family clutched to their chests, and sob their way towards oblivion.

You don't know what type you are. You just want to give things up: sugar, cigarettes, beer, television, work, love, life. You breathe onto the glass and draw a smiling face. Maybe that makes you a Forsakavist. It sounds Russian. It sounds good. As you smile into the glass you think of how a psychiatrist would most probably say you are crazy. Well, maybe not crazy, but he'd have some fancy university word that meant the same thing.

Shrinks they are called in America and that sounds about right to you because every time you meet one you feel diminished. In many ways you feel sorry for them because all psychiatrists end up infected with the mental illness they hope to treat anyway. Just like all cardiologists end up dying of broken hearts and plastic surgeons wake up one day and don't recognise the face looking back at them in the mirror. But as you stare in the mirror you do recognise the face looking back. You recognise it just fine. It is you: James Fitzhenry and you are giving up. Then, as you stroke that beard, you remember that you've one more thing to do.

So you're sitting in the café looking at the wicker chair. You smell bad and you look bad. Women sprayed scent as soon as you sat down. As they left you watched those perfumed particles hanging heavy in the afternoon air. The waitress comes and lays down a pot of tea before you and a slice of Madeira cake. You nod and wait for her to walk away. But you hear the legs screech as she sits down in the wicker seat opposite you, the chair that no one sits in because it's your sister's. By now you're too weak to feel offended so you watch as her bony painted fingers tear open the wrapper around your sister's cake. Then you see her slice it into small pieces with a bread knife. When she's done she slides the saucer across the table. 'Eat it,' she says.

'It's my sister's,' you tell her and you slide the saucer back.

'Eat it,' she tells you and this time she keeps her hand on the china plate to stop you from moving it.

You pick the first piece up and chew. And it must look terrible the way you're eating, with your mouth open, feral, crumbs spiked onto the bristles of your beard. But it tastes so good and she doesn't seem bothered so you take another piece. She takes a packet of cigarettes from her pocket and lights one. She draws her cheeks in as she inhales, unblinking eyes on you as she slides the packet and lighter across to your side of the table. You take one out and light it. She pours tea into your cup.

You take out your notepad and ask her for her full name. She tells you it's Stacey Phillips. You try to find a meaningful anagram and you can't. You begin to panic.

'Do you have a middle name?' you ask her.

'No,' she says, and she tips the sugar into your cup.

# 'I and Thou'

*Alison Scott*

Like the sick rush of too much salt and wine
the ship goes down.

Lately I've taken to stumbling
down in the night, the kitchen
still, the shadows outside. Filling
the kettle in the half dark. The clenching,

cramping fear of other people how
they can destroy, pecking like crows at the
soft underbelly. Or, how the crowds
who gather to watch the stoning
to see the hard eyes, hear
the shrill voices, stay and are drawn
down, to be in the centre of that. Or,

as when a child, first being tickled, unsure,
laughs to appease with frightened eyes,
(as the fingers claw and poke)
from then fears the turning
of the world, knowing how it can,
in a moment's breath.

# Pipes

*Ciara MacLaverty*

It must be some kind of sign
that I want to dive in
and find you in this poem
rather than wait
until the poem finds you.

Where, where are you, in pipes?
Then, through frustrations
of paling memory,
I find you in the dairy
in T-shirt and Welly boots.
Milk sloshes above us
in long glass tubes:
shocked waves of white,
going wherever it goes.

Fine hairs on your arms
stand up - there are no doors
to shield wind, rain or
anyone who might catch us
kissing; so we don't, but it is there
in the swing of my hips,
the tilt of your head
and the hiss and suck of the pumps.

Forgive me for falling back here.
I'm a grown woman,
more content than I ever expected to be.
It's only the siphoning of a glad heart,
milking years of
luck upon luck
never wanting to spill a drop.

# Broken

*Beth McDonough*

This is the body he
didn't want; the one he quit
too soon. Here she is, shaped
by that fullmoon night when all
the world's waters coursed
her legs and already she knew
she'd failed him.

# My Grandmother's Commonplace Book

*Henry Bell*

August sixth in blue ink and
scored across the yellow page
like notes
are three exclamation marks.
Each one fainter:
the first cuts straight down,
the next two curling up;
not into a question
but the other way, like a foetus.
Before them the words
Atomic Bomb
!

!

!

# Flute song

*Judith Taylor*

I'm tired of playing the sweet girl
with the silvery, cheerful voice

the lilting bird tone
that is so reliably brightening

when I could be low
insinuating

muscular
as a serpent

my sidelong trail in the dust
your only indication

where I've been.
I could be bleak

and hazardous: knives
glitter too; poisons flow.

To produce those dancing phrases
you delight in

I use force: I make
hard, disciplined air.

You know to fear me
when I'm thirty strong, with drums

– do you think all that comes out of nowhere?
Do you ever think

when you hand me another part
as a babbling ingenue

you could push your luck
too far? That you could one day ask a girl

to be just that last degree
too light, and bright, and sparkling?

# Me with 'Juggler', 1952

*Kathrine Sowerby*

I'm fifteen, standing in the garden.
The creases in my shirt cast shadows.
Lupins point to the top of the fence,
their leaves splayed like fingers.

Juggler is far from finished,
her wings are fragile skeletons.
Her motor is held with elastic bands,
her balsa wood still nude.

I'll fly her over the washing,
over the neighbour sunbathing,
a book held at arm's length,
shielding his eyes from the sun.

# Anne and 'Pacer', 1953

*Kathrine Sowerby*

Anne is in soft focus.
The fence runs at an angle.
Her hair is moulded off her face,
tucked behind her ears.

She holds Pacer for me.
The wing rests on her shoulder.
The number that I painted,
the cockpit that I glued.

The trees are bare in the background.
Their twigs blanch into sky.
The heavy pleats of Anne's tweed skirt
blow against her knees.

# Faun

*Janette Ayachi*

The boys from Inverleith schools
seem more interested in each other
than the chewing gum-smiles of girls,
old men kick up leaves in these streets
dreaming of the goat-smell of locker rooms.

# Bring Me the Head of John Logie Baird

*Graham Fulton*

*Mr Watson Come here I want to see you*
were the first words spoken
by Alexander Graham Bell
right after he'd invented
the easy payment swipe screen smart phone
with full infinity access to hardcore pornography,
but as there's no statue of him in Scotland
I'll go to see the bust of John Logie Baird instead
who invented the 90 inch ceiling-dangling
fibre optic high definition controlled-by-a-chip-
inserted-in-your-brain-at-birth television
in Helensburgh,
but he's in a right state
as they're removing the esplanade
to make way for a crazy golf course
designed by Charles Rennie Mackintosh,
and all that's left of his pioneering spectacles
is the bridge welded to his nose
because maybe he's been watching
too much telly.
and it appears he's had his fill of modern life,
the choices, the unlimitations,
but seems quite content
as he gazes chubbily out
over the low tide Clyde
with only the no-nonsense clouds
moving unhurriedly from right to left,
the big sun coming and going,
and the mad gulls bouncing from clump to clump
of brown seaweed which looks like billions
of the top halves of hairy human heads
with the rest of the body submerged
and no way to change the channel

# What This Place Needs

*Dilys Rose*

Brenda has lost her luggage. No, the airline she flew with has lost it and she is out of sorts. She is on the U-Bahn on the way into the city centre of Nuremberg with no clothes other than what she has on. Not even, for a four day stint, a spare pair of big black emergency knickers in her hand luggage. A careless oversight. No makeup or toiletries either, other than the permitted 100 ml. squirt of toothpaste. In the compartment, two sleepy children nuzzle against their silent mother, two African men in identical jerseys nod in time to music on their iPods, and a woman, large like herself, is knitting something dainty and fiddly. There's a smell of pickle and the burnt rubber of brake linings.

In the morning she will have to shop, return to her hotel, change into a new, untested outfit, go on the tour then give her presentation. Brenda hates shopping in foreign cities. She hates shopping in a hurry. It's never easy to find clothes which fit, never mind flatter. Though all she really needs for her presentation is on her laptop, on her memory stick or in her head, she is a firm believer that a good delivery requires a good outfit.

The clothes she has been wearing for the last twelve hours – loose black trousers and long, concealing top – have lost their artful casualness: they're crumpled, floppy, give off whiffs of airline food and sweat. She has no deodorant or cologne – it was that or toothpaste – never mind a powder compact to blot her shiny nose. The credit note from the airline will just about cover one outfit and personal requisites for the next 24 hours. If, after that, her suitcase is still missing, she will receive full compensation for the value of her luggage. But why would she want to buy a whole new travel wardrobe when it has taken years to put together a colour-coordinated set of long loose tops and trousers in black, aubergine, chocolate? There is still a slim chance that her suitcase will be delivered to her hotel later tonight or even tomorrow morning, and that all will then be well.

Stepping off the escalator from the U-Bahn, Brenda's first sight of the city is a cobbled square, dominated by a mediaeval *kirche* and *turm*. The place is all but deserted. A young woman with long, flaxen plaits and a drindl skirt pushes a bicycle past the *kirche:* on the handlebars is a wicker basket festooned with silk flowers and plastic greenery. Quaint, in a kitschy way. A thin man with twisted feet hirples across the empty expanse of cobbles. Not so quaint. The striped Punch and Judy awnings of the bratwurst stalls are buttoned down for the night.

The sky is a plush blue, deepening. A sliver of moon hangs behind the tip of the *kirche* steeple. The moon appears to quiver, like a shiny weighing pan settling into equilibrium. It is so quiet, she can hear herself breathe; her lungs sound like creaky bellows. Without her suitcase, she feels unusually light; she imagines rising from the cobbles and floating around the church spire in the manner of a Zeppelin. But Zeppelins are too early. By the time Hitler had begun to stage his mass rallies, Zeppelins had had their day. And when the time came, the city was bombed by Spitfires.

Her grandfather, a wartime pilot, told her this, with a touch of pride, when she mentioned that Nuremberg was her next destination. He fetched the photo from the mantelpiece in the care home. The mantelpiece was purely decorative, no open fires were allowed. He waved the faded photo in front of her, the same photo he showed her every time she visited; a portrait of him in goggles and flying jacket, young and brave and handsome.

Ninety per cent of Nuremberg was destroyed! he whispered loudly in her ear, as though it were a state secret. Ninety per cent! Then with a tight, anxious grin, took himself to the window and stared up at the sky. Cirrus, he'd said. Still snow in the air. Mind and wrap up.

She crosses the square, walks down a street dotted with barely lit *love bars* and lap dancing joints, turns and finds herself in a narrow, deserted alley. On one side is the high dark perimeter wall, on the other a strip of pink-lit plate-glass windows. When visitors see the phrase, 'in the heart of the old town', as she will point out during her presentation, they don't usually equate this with the red light district. To properly direct footfall, tourists need more accurate information.

In the tourist business Brenda is considered to be a leading advisor on how to rebrand places with a chequered history. She has met numerous dignitaries world-wide; she has witnessed countless renderings of indigenous music, dance and cultural ceremonies; she has chewed and even recklessly swallowed every kind of national delicacy, from the weird to the disgusting to the potentially deadly. She finds it difficult not to preface her cache of traveller's tales with: When I was in Caracas, Beirut, Kabul...

It's by no means the first time she has turned a corner in an unfamiliar city and found herself faced with an array of hookers displaying their wares but bang up against the city wall, in buildings which must once have been stables, with horses nodding long velvety heads, snuffling into straw and waiting to be put to work, seems an odd location.

Once she's out of the red light district, she continues through empty streets until she reaches a little old square near the river: on one corner stands a traditional toyshop – and toys, she remembers, are something else for which Nuremberg is famous. The window is crammed with puppets and character dolls: Pinocchio, Hansel and Gretel, Rapunzel, Little Red Cap, who is accompanied by a fun fur wolf. Does the wolf open up? Does it have a zip on its underbelly from which the gobbled up grandmother can pop out? Brenda has never liked fairy tales: too much violence, weirdness.

She crosses the river by a narrow bridge. A lopsided gingerbread cottage clings to the far end. Above it, a sign in gothic lettering reads: *The Hangman's Museum: See how the hangman really lived! 5 Euro.* Along the riverbank other quaint, ancient buildings sag against each other. Sweet-voiced birds are flying home to roost. A willow dips its branches in the water. She might have stepped back several centuries, to a time long before the history that put the place on the map. But if ninety per cent of the city was destroyed, how much of this olde worlde Nuremberg is genuine?

Her hotel, when she finds it, at the end of a rather drab street, is clean, functional and bland: straight lines, subdued colours, subdued musak, silk flowers in tall, dry vases. Her travel allowance would have covered somewhere more upmarket but Brenda makes a point of booking cheap or mid-price rooms; you need to stay in touch with the bread and butter of the industry. That's one reason. Another is that if you keep your expenses down, you're more likely to be asked back.

The room itself is adequate but by no means luxurious. No bathrobes are provided and the towels are far from ample. Under other circumstances the lack of bathrobe or the size of towels wouldn't have mattered but even if she had time to have what she is wearing laundered – which she doesn't – what could she have done if the fire alarm went off?

She orders a sandwich from room service, munches as she skims through her presentation notes, then, to attune her ear to the languages, switches on the TV. Nobody expects her to say more than a few words in German – English is, after all, the *lingua franca* of tourism – but she likes to make an effort. The programmes are mostly intense talk shows, banal game shows, grim, grainy monochrome footage on the history channels, and soft porn.

She's annoyed at herself for staying in her room like some timid tourist, lacking enough sense of adventure to broach the threshold of a local hostrelry, one of those places with trestle tables and blazing hearths where she could order up a plate of smoky sausages and potato salad, knock back a stein of beer and sink into noisy joviality. She could call Nora, suggest a nightcap but hates to appear needy.

Brenda knows a great many people in the industry and meets new people all the time. But work trips tend to be short and swift, over and done with before anything has a chance to develop. In her line of work, you have to act on first impressions, steel yourself to make your way into, through and, if need be, out the side door of function rooms filled with strangers. You have to form instant alliances, to waste no time in finding a temporary soul-mate, or at least somebody you can bear to spend an evening with. You have to be able to handle farewells with dignity, or wit, or speed.

The winter before last, she first ran into Nora, in Reykjavik. The two of them spent a glittering snowy evening eating herring and drinking vodka. Nora, wee Nora, with her pixie haircut and geeky specs, her tweedy sack of a skirt and granny cardigan – brisk, bossy, no-nonsense Nora escorted her back to her hotel, wrapped her in a bony little hug then set off, unsteadily, down the snow-packed road to her own hotel.

Tomorrow, Nora will also be delivering a presentation. She and Brenda work for rival companies. Both are keen to secure a contract, any contract. Tour companies are going under faster than you can say exchange rate. Along with your sun, sea and sex, along with your culture, your traditional, nouveau and fusion cuisine and however many wonders of the world, there's quite a bit more to throw into the pot: keeping up with outbreaks of crime or contagious diseases; fluctuations in the stock market, natural disasters, political uprisings,any one of which can flare up and wreak holidaymaker havoc. Can a lass from Luton who left school at sixteen be expected to have a strategy to deal with situations that entire governments fail to get a handle on?

She and Nora were in Reykjavik when Eyjafjallajokull erupted and a dust cloud covered most of the northern hemisphere. Iceland's banks were on the brink of collapse – or had they already collapsed? Brenda is already fuzzy about the order of events. She tries to keep up with international affairs but there's just too much going on, too many places where newsworthy things are happening. It didn't take long, she does remember, before the frothy, optimistic conference presentations hit a layer of permafrost gloom.

Nora's presentation for Reykjavik was provocatively entitled: *What this Place Doesn't Need*. She suggested that there might be other ways to introduce international, short stay visitors to the culture than serving up a sheep's head on a plate, or a portion of fermented shark, with its distinctive, punch in the gut aroma. Appreciating such delicacies, Nora pointed out, took years, generations. Strange food, sky-high prices and then a dust-spewing volcano which succeeded in bringing air transport to a standstill for weeks was not a winning combination. Not much you could do about a volcano but you could rethink your menu. The Icelandic hosts didn't get Nora's jokes. They spikily defended their cuisine and, when the dark, volcanic chocolate cake and coffee was served up, they pointedly ignored her. Nora laughed it off but she'd been glad of Brenda's company that night, glad to have somebody to hit the vodka with.

After filling up on a healthy Nuremberg breakfast buffet – fresh fruit salad, cold cuts and cheese, rustic bread and jewel-coloured jams and honeys – Brenda makes for the main shopping area, a grid of thoroughly swept, pedestrianised streets. Blue sky. Sunshine. The shop windows gleam. A department store advertises *Das Mollig Kollektion*. It even has a window display of *mollig* mannequins, with moulded Marcel waves which set them back half a century. The mannequins are clad in tops and trousers in Easter basket colours: primrose, crocus, duck-egg blue.

Optimistically she takes the sleek, humming elevator to the third floor. She is impressed by the extent of the collection – an entire *mollig* floor! – but there's not a single black garment in sight, nor anything in chocolate or aubergine; every garment yodels *spring*! What do people do if they need something subdued, for a job interview, say, or a funeral? Or because they need to go to court, or to be quizzed about a wayward child by a head teacher or social worker?

Today, *nicht schwarz*, says the *mollig* assistant. She is wearing the store uniform, a short, tight-fitting aqua dress, with yellow polkadots, and a glossy, *mollig* smile. Colour *gut,* she says. Colour beautiful. The assistant pulls out a selection of outfits. Strong solid colours, broad stripes or busy floral prints. How should Brenda choose between them? Would she rather be a tent, a deckchair or an overgrown garden?

Try. *Gut.* Beautiful, says the beaming shop assistant then spins on her neat, aqua heels, leaving Brenda to the hot bright intimacy of the changing room.

Most of the stuff she tries on is hopeless, though the fabrics are crisp and light and the cut is generous, but there's one outfit she tries on a second time: a grass green trouser suit printed with giant daisies. She can't help smiling at her reflection; she looks vernal, festive, frivolous.

So! says the shop assistant, ringing up the total. The till has a cheery chirp. *Gut!* Beautiful!

After she has also purchased some underwear, a pair of green leather shoes – has she ever before owned green shoes? – a cherry red lipstick and some other essential toiletries, she hurries back to the hotel, oddly excited. She requests her key at reception. The trim young desk girl stops her:

*Bitte*, Madame. Your baggage has just now arrived!

Oh, she says. Good. But I'm in a hurry. Could you keep my case at reception until this evening?

*Ja?* says the girl, shaking her head, adjusting her spectacles. If you wish.

Brenda is not in that much of a hurry. She just doesn't want to have to make any further decisions about what to wear, or consider any ironing. While she was out shopping her room has already been cleaned, the bed made up. Two discs of chocolate nestle on the pillows. She pulls off yesterday's clothes and wriggles into the daisy suit. Can she really go through with this new loud look? Will it undermine her professional reputation for evermore? A bird lands on the window ledge and twitters gaily as she slips on her new shoes and slaps on some bold red lipstick.

Though she has done her homework on the not inconsequential history of the city, she likes to spend a few hours walking around a place, getting a feel for the locale, noting down some up-to-the-minute, first-hand details to give her presentation an edge. Today there's no time for that; she'll have to make do with her memory stick and a new, untried and untested outfit.

At the Doku Centrum terminus, a welcome party awaits, to a man and woman in neutral monochrome suits, ironed expressions, manicured hair, clutching their iPads and other state-of-the-art Notebooks. Even Nora looks alarmingly crease free and soberly attired, apart from a pair of huge hooped earrings which resemble snapped handcuffs. As Brenda steps down onto the immaculate platform, enjoying the demure sound of the tram door gliding shut behind her, she senses a communal flicker of... surprise, disapproval?

I am Gisela, says a sleek blonde with Dietrich cheekbones. So, we are now complete.

As Brenda is a few minutes late, though only a few minutes, nothing to get worked up about – and Gisela is pointedly looking at her watch – she doesn't stop to worry too much about what the welcome party thinks of her outfit. In fact, she doesn't feel like worrying at all. In her loud print gear she might be a tourist herself, just nipping out of town on the super-efficient public transport system for a quick, edifying trip, a sobering fact-finding trip, undoubtedly, but a trip all the same.

Out of the city centre, there's a cool breeze, a sharp, gritty smell in the air, like steel dust. A bank of dark cloud is rolling in.

So, says Gisela, before we go into the Docu Centrum, we will take a tour of the outside.

Obediently the delegates follow her along a gravel path between straggly bushes.

Bit of a schlep, this venue.

Yeah. And do we really want to see it?

The Rathaus has a lot more going for it as a venue.

Yeah. Haven't they done wonders with the town centre!

A labour of love, these reconstruction jobs. Have you seen Gdansk? Warsaw?

We will walk about, says Gisela.

They pass a small, dull lake and a ramshackle fairground, not yet open for business. Without the romance of the night, of blaring music and strings of coloured lights, the painted rides look shabby. Alsatians pad back and forth, jangle their chains. There's a lingering whiff of fried onions and candy floss.

Dig the outfit, says Nora.

Not too frivolous?

Nah, says Nora, putting a flame to her roll-up. Cheery.

As they walk around the rather boring parkway, Brenda catches sight of her green and white legs, the banks of green and white daisies swaying as she follows Gisela's determined lead along the path. Gisela is not walking at a tourist pace. She would not, Brenda thinks, make a good tour guide. A tourist pace is a languid amble, as if there's all the time in the world to go where you're going, or to simply stand and stare. Gisela is goading, not guiding.

People never take tourists seriously. Not even the people who make their living from tourists. They're always considered to be a bit ridiculous, pathetic, desperate, looking for something beyond themselves which they can absorb, consume, assimilate, something they can sniff or stroke or swallow, and after a bit of somewhere else they can't wait to get back to their own beds, to draw the curtains on life elsewhere and sink into the warm amniotic bath of what they know, and so don't have to think about. As if that's wrong. As if they're all just brainless sponges.

So, says Gisela, now you see where it happened.

As they round a bend in the path they come upon the rally ground, a great man-made maw. None of the delegates is prepared for the scale of the place, its palpable air of dereliction. Unused for seventy years, weeds push through the cracks in the concrete, the brick walls are discoloured, crumbling. In such a vast, barren space, the small cluster of delegates makes no more impression than a few specks of grit, flakes of ash. In this gigantic parade ground, how many thousands, in unison, saluted and screamed *Seig Heil*?

This is part of history, says Gisela, we have to live with.

Dark tourism's on the up.

Yeah. Tours to Beirut, Ground Zero, Cambodia's killing fields. Auschwitz is old news – Gisela flinches at the mention of Auschwitz.

I am hoping, says Gisela, that today's guest speakers bring some good ideas.

Gisela draws the delegates' attention to Brenda and Nora who are lagging a bit behind the rest of the group. A tall, grey-clad man takes a photo of them on his phone. Others follow suit; snap the odd couple, the weirdos.

Smile, says Brenda.

No way, says Nora. She scowls for the cameras, skins up prison rolly, lights up and sucks on it aggressively.

So, says Gisela. Now we go inside.

For an hour or more Gisela escorts them through archive footage: swarms of swastikas and jackboots, massed armies and piles of corpses, bombed-out cities and chisel-jawed stormtroopers, *Blitzkreig* and *Kristallnacht,* a screaming madman whose last planned rally, before invading Poland, was to have been on the theme of peace.

Are we getting lunch before the presentations?

Hope so. Breakfast wasn't much cop.

Mine was okay. Rubbish coffee, though.

Tried the famous sausages yet?

No. How about tonight? Sample the beer too.

Goes without saying.

We have much film footage, says Gisela. Many newsreels. We do not pretend the past did not happen. We teach our schoolchildren about the mistakes of the past. But for the city to survive, we must have something else to offer.

It is with relief that the delegates exit the dark, crowded walls of Doku Centrum exhibition hall to gather in the glass-walled concourse where screens and a podium have been set up for the power point presentations. The delegates take their seats. There is no sign of food or refreshments. Brenda is up first.

The crisp cotton of her loud, frivolous outfit rustles she moves her arms; it's a pleasant, fresh sound, like grasses shifting in the breeze. She has become too used to the dry crackle of static, of stay-press synthetics, of dark acquisitive colours which suck light into themselves.

At Gisela's signal, Brenda prepares to approach the podium.

I hope you've got some good ideas, Nora hisses.

# Glenhead

*Kirsty Gunn*

Anyhow she was fed up with him. Sneezing and coughing and pulling out that dark handkerchief that looked as though it had been balled in his pocket for weeks. It was revolting. And the children were revolted, her children. What was she doing with him, anyway? What on earth?

'Mum?'

Some relationships might be ok for a night or two, an affair, even, for a while... But not in a car together, now. Not this.

'What?'

Not this driving off to look at some house in the countryside somewhere when she'd promised the children they would always be city children, that they would always belong in town.

'I'm hungry.'

'I know,' Sarah said. 'Me, too. We'll stop soon, promise. We'll find somewhere for lunch.'

Because, stability. That's what everyone said children needed, wasn't it? The importance of keeping some semblance of the same routine, the same life. The sense of the day to day having gone on uninterrupted, no matter what happened. You didn't force big changes, not even now, not even after a year had passed. You kept everything calm. Schools. The house. Just have everything stay the same...

For the sake of the children.

'Promise?'

Isn't that what everybody said?

'I promise,' Sarah replied. 'Somewhere really nice, with puddings and everything. I promise, darling.'

It is what everybody said.

But who knew, really, what children thought or needed? You just didn't. Like now, with Tim driving and her sitting beside him like a wife. That wasn't anything like routine, was it? Yet, lunch. Being hungry. That seemed to account for most of what the children were thinking now. There was Nicky with his headphones on and Elsa had asked to have some track or other and now they were listening together, Elsa singing quietly along to the song like she was just a little girl.

Trying to drown out, probably, the sound of Tim's ghastly trumpeting and wheezing.

'You really are unwell,' Sarah said, looking out of the window, away from him.

'I know you hate it'. Tim moved his hand, the one without the handkerchief, onto her thigh.

She didn't reply. But neither did she move his hand. She let it sit there, on her leg, like a creature that one feels sorry for.

'Don't worry. I'm feeling better,' Tim said. It's a British thing. I swear I never used to get sick at all back in the States.'

Outside, the countryside was flattened into winter, flat brown fields, low brown hills, brown river. The trees were massed in clumps beneath a grey sky and they looked like they were made of nothing more, Sarah thought, than bits of wire, sticking here, sticking there. There'd never be any sap to those branches, no green. Earth formed ridges along the farmland at the side of the road and sheep and cattle stood motionless in the cold. Every now and then a quick brittle wind disturbed the image of it all, the dull landscape, shook it into life. But for the most part nothing moved except her car and Tim driving, coughing, blowing into that handkerchief again.

'I'd say we're about five minutes away...' Sarah had the estate agent's details on the dashboard in front of her, and took another quick look at the map on the back of the glossy folder. 'It says here, take the turn off the B768 and follow signs for Glenbank...Oh, hang on – '

At that second she saw the sign up ahead.

'It's right there. We're here after all.'

Tim slowed down. There was no sign of any house, though. No gate or any sort of entrance.

'Mum'.

Nicky had flipped out his ear plug and was leaning forward into the front seat.

'This is a total waste of time,' he said.

So there it was again, stability, see? People had talked about it for months, they still talked about it. That the children were at the age when you had to be careful. No alterations to the day-to-day. No life style shifts.

'A total waste,' Nicky said again.

Sarah could hear the music he was playing buzzing out of the tiny plug dangled around his neck. God knows how loud he'd had it turned up. Elsa was still listening. She had her hand up to her ear holding the little earpiece in place and was mouthing the words now, no longer singing.

Stability. Stability.

'Mum?'

'Can you turn off that thing for a minute, please? I can't hear myself think.' Sarah picked up the glossy brochure, put it down again.

'I don't want to do this either', said Elsa, her voice without expression. 'I'm still hungry, though,' she said. 'I could still eat.'

Teenagers. They were teenagers, after all. Still, this was awful for them. Sarah knew that. She acknowledged. The whole thing, the car. Tim. Tim driving. Sneezing. Tim himself sitting there next to their mother in the car, the family car. Tim who'd stayed the night the night before, who'd stayed many nights… Awful for teenagers, the whole thing. Awful.

'Mum?'

And now here was Tim with her, with them, in the middle of nowhere. An estate agent's brochure on the dashboard… They knew something was up. Of course they did. Though she hadn't said a word about the house, about what she and Tim had been discussing, a fresh start, all of that. God no. She'd just said, 'Let's go to the country for lunch,' that's all. 'And look, we might see this house on the way.' 'What house?' And she'd shown Elsa the details in the brochure, the big rooms, the stable for a pony. 'But I like our house,' Elsa had said. 'I don't want to move anywhere else.' 'I know, I know. But let's just have a nice drive, ok?'

So yes, it was awful for them. In their own car with their mother's boyfriend driving. Even that word, though Sarah had never used it. 'Boyfriend'. Because that's what everyone said, didn't they? After a divorce and they'd met someone new? No matter how old, people called him a boyfriend. Mostly they did, or 'someone new'.

And Nicky and Elsa had to be with 'someone new', their mother's 'boyfriend'… God, Sarah felt ill with it. What was she doing? What? Yet here they were, in the middle of nowhere, driving off to see a house that they all might… What? Live in? Was that really the plan? What on earth was she thinking?'

'It's going to be great,' Tim said. And touched her thigh again. 'Look around us, all. It's beautiful here.'

But was it? Really? On one level. Sarah could see, through Tim's, through an American's eyes… The Scottish countryside, all that. Rural Perthshire, and only an hour from Edinburgh… Who could say Perthshire wasn't lovely? But now? With its brown hills? In this cold?

'Beautiful,' said Tim again. Though he didn't say 'beautiful'. BeauDiful's what he said. With his American accent. With his cold. Not beautiful at all. Nothing was.

They turned off the little road up the private drive. There was still no sign of the actual house. It was like turning into a field, the drive just a swathe of dark cut into the earth, through the tall dry sedge that bordered it. In summer all this would be green. In summer… Sarah thought. When would that ever be? In summer when all this land around would be cut for hay and golden green? When the trees up ahead, that she could see now, would be in full leaf and casting a lovely purple shade across the lawn that came now fully into view, in front of a large grey house and the glimpse of a river, beside.

'Deserves its name alright!' Tim said, delighted. 'Doesn't it? Look! Behind? That'll be the glen, right? And the river here beside it? Come on –' he'd stopped the car, turned off the engine. 'Let's have a look!'

He reached down at Sarah's feet and pulled up a jacket.

'This will be fun!'

For a second, Sarah had a glimpse of that boyish charm she'd been so attracted to, when was it... six months ago? After Alastair had left. This will be fun, he'd said then, too, when they'd met at a cocktail party and he'd invited her there, straightaway, out for supper at some really fancy place. And it had been, fun, hadn't it? Then? When she'd needed some fun? She'd thought so at the time, anyway...

Now he walked off away from her, putting on his jacket as he went, opening the gate and leaving it wide, stopping, Sarah saw, to pull the wretched handkerchief out again. Yet he was good looking, wasn't he? Tall, with that American build from playing lots of sport. They all played football, didn't they, American football and it made them tall like that, with those broad shoulders... Everyone had said he was good looking. Now he stopped to blow his nose and cast his gaze around the house and its gardens. Master of all he surveyed, is what he would be thinking. Just beauDiful. This damn country. Ah, Scotland. The fishing. The stalking. The life of the gentleman. The whole damn thing.

'Come on!' he shouted back to them. He blew his nose again and gestured to her. 'Come on, you all!'

'I'm not getting out of the car,' Nicky said. Elsa was looking out of the window, away from the house, away from her mother's boyfriend. Nicky had both his earplugs back in and his eyes were closed, his mind full of music.

Neither of them needing her.

Is what Sarah had been telling herself, more and more, these past weeks. Because teenagers... What teenagers needed their mothers anyway? And those routines everybody talked about, their mothers' routines? All that stability, where did that get you, anyway? Teenagers themselves wouldn't want any part of a routine, they were unstable, that was the whole point of being a teenager. And any moment they'd be grown up and gone and she would be on her own. She would be alone and they would be living somewhere else, and maybe far away...Or, she'd thought, alternatively, as she'd been telling herself, being rational, thinking about the future, she could be with someone. Someone new. After all, Alastair had been gone for a year now, nothing was going to change, was it? He wasn't coming back.

Suddenly Sarah was exhausted. The weather. The brown, damp earth. Probably coming down with something, Tim's damn cold. Everything felt shivery. Even with the car heater turned on and up and raging away, she wanted to hunch down in her seat, go deep into herself, deep in...

Tim had gone. She couldn't see him, he must be around the back. She'd give him a few more minutes and then, ok, she'd get out of the car, she'd go and join him. Have a look around the house like he wanted her to. After all, it was pretty enough. A square Georgian façade giving on to a flat green lawn. Long clear windows. It would be lovely inside. Sarah knew that, without even having to imagine it.

That's why she'd said, 'Why not?' when Tim had shown her the brochure and suggested coming out here. One dead weekend in late January...And by now they'd been seeing each other long enough that Nicky and Elsa were used to him, surely?

'You never know,' Tim had said. 'Kids. They love a fresh start like the rest of us. Nicky could have a shed for his drums, Elsa could get a horse if she wants one. I'd buy her a horse.'

So...

BeauDiful.

But still they always said, didn't they, the experts? That children needed continuity after divorce? And that women needed to wait, the mothers did, until the flak from the split had settled, before they made any changes? Because the children needed time to come to terms with it, that Daddy's not coming home. They needed time and so everything had to wait until then, until when they'd grown up a little. Stopped believing in happy endings.

Sarah reached in the back for her jacket, rumpled between the two of them, her children, like a soft, soft old blanket.

'Our children,' she and Alastair had said once. She couldn't look at them now.

Quickly, she shoved the jacket on and got out of the car, but then, just for a second, caught Elsa's eye. Just for a second, but it was dead, the look her daughter gave back to her. Like the countryside around her. Nothing was alive there.

'Leave the engine on, mum,' Elsa said. 'So we can have the radio. If you're getting out of the car, I want the radio on. The music we have is too quiet.'

'No it's not,' Sarah said to her. 'I could hear it from the front seat, blaring through your earphones.'

'Well believe me, mother. I couldn't hear a thing. Not with your boyfriend sneezing.'

'He's not my boyfriend. Tim is not a boy.'

'You know what I mean, Sarah.'

'He's sure as hell not my Dad,' Nicky said. 'I know that much.'

'Atish-hoo! – Atish-hoo! We all fall down,' Elsa sang.

In a second, Nicky was out of the car and running. He didn't have a jersey on.

'Wait!' Sarah called out to him. 'We can look at the house together!'

'He doesn't want to look at your bloody house,' said Elsa.

Outside, the air was even colder than she'd thought. And damp. She could breathe it, that deep clammy breath of an old, old kind of cold. Sarah was shivering with it. It was in her bones, in her blood it felt like. Christ, she was freezing. So what was going on here? That she would still be holding out here, right now, standing here? Imagining herself in a house she had no intention of living in? Did she? With a man she did not want to be with? With children who looked at her the way Elsa had just looked at her. It was dead everywhere, this place. There was no relief.

Even so, still shivering, her whole body, she walked away from the car with no intention of following her son, still she walked around the side of the house and Tim was there, just standing, peering into a window. Not part of any of these thoughts of her own, he was doing nothing. Well, he was blowing his nose.

So – 'We all fall down...' Sarah sang the line to herself.

'Shame,' he called out to her when he was finished, the handkerchief back in the pocket of his ugly green parka. 'There's been a cock up with the keys. They're not where the agent said he'd leave them. We can't get in to see the place after all.'

'Oh.'

Sarah was looking in a back window through to a scullery and kitchen. Clearly the house hadn't been lived in for years. There was an old butcher's sink in the room, nothing else. She went to the other window at the same back extension, it gave on to a little hallway. All was dark there. Overall, the house was smaller than she'd thought, than it seemed. The agent's details had it looking quite expansive and when they'd turned in to the lawn it was even grand. But not really. Not now that she was close up. It was a bit of a disaster, actually. Like the phrase Tim had just used, that sounded so strange in his American mouth, 'cock up'. That was what this place amounted to, their visit here, her being in the car with someone she didn't love, had never loved, with her children who were her children, her and Alistair's children...

'You're right, there's been a cock up,' she said to Tim now. 'It's an awful house. No wonder it's derelict. No wonder it's so cheap.'

'You call this cheap?' Tim said. 'Jesus. I'd like to know what you call expensive. The place is gorgeous, it's got great atmosphere. I looked in the front, there's a staircase goes way up to –'

'Who cares?' Sarah knew she was being mean. 'It just has fake grandeur, that's all. It's not a real house, not for a real family to live in. It's just someone's idea of showing off...'

'What?' Poor Tim. He was all confused. All the sleeping with him, all the talking and discussions. All the letting him stay over, letting him do that more and more. Having him spend weekends, even, getting to know the children, letting him drive her car...

'I don't know what you're talking about,' he said. 'Jesus, Sarah...'

'Well, look,' she said to him, he'd started walking away. 'Look at this house,' she said. 'There is no glen to be head of, don't you see? Just a bit of a river... It's flat, Tim, there are no hills here, no glens...'

She was talking to herself, really. Tim had left her to it. He was heading back to the car,

'There's no point in staying here,' he called to her over his shoulder. 'We'll have to come back with keys.'

'Don't be silly,' Sarah said. The words formed a frosty breath in front of her face, eve though she'd spoken so quietly. They'd never be back. She went around the side of the house, still looking in windows, and then to the front. There, true, Tim had been right, the house seemed to regain itself. There was the dining room, a hall, the interior door open so she could see light from a fanlight cast across the parquet floor, the turn of a banister...

'Oh, you're pretty enough,' Sarah said. 'So why are you so alone?'

'Because the man I loved left me,' the house replied. 'He doesn't love me and he's gone away. And I have no heart,' the house whispered. 'Only empty rooms, and most of them are cramped and dark...'

Sarah turned away from the window and looked over towards the car. Nicky was standing there by the open back door, Elsa huddled inside. The radio was blaring, awful, awful music with a tinny, electric beat. What were they thinking, her children? Of her? Of this day? Were they thinking about their father, who they loved, or their father's girlfriend who they had met a number of times and now Alastair was talking about them all going on holiday together, him and them together, and his girlfriend, too? Were they thinking about that, about holidays, or only of this, this cold now, where they were, this minute, this brown, brown earth? Only thinking about nothing at all? At her back, the house waited, like her own shadow. Sarah felt its presence, the poor thing. It didn't know either. They were both of them just waiting. Sitting there, with their empty rooms but the door shut tight and locked.

For a second, Sarah wanted to turn and go back. Try and find another way in, break a window. Tell Tim she'd found a loose door back there in the scullery and could he force it. Tell him that they could find a way to get in to the ground floor through the cellar, maybe, a separate entrance, somehow, someway, so that she could step into that lovely hall, feel the light from the fan window upon her face, let the house admit her. She would mount the wide stairs then, enter all the rooms and who knows, yes, maybe stay there as Tim had talked about, yes, maybe buy the house and live there and maybe Tim would be her husband and Nicky and Elsa, they would have another father as well as Alastair and in time, all four of them, all four adults could be here together, in summer, the trees in leaf, the fields green, and they would be having lunch together, all of them here, and the children too, and drinks out on the lawn...

But that was crazy. Everything. What was she thinking? The house – it wasn't a real house. She'd seen that already, without needing to turn back to it, to check it again, she knew, the house knew. It was a fake. Where was Tim, anyway? They needed to be getting on. The children hadn't moved. They were still waiting there by the car, Nicky leaning against it, so tall now, like his father. The music would hold them, Sarah supposed, as long as they wanted it to, they would leave it playing. They were teenagers, after all. What was any of this to them that they should even be thinking about it?

'I promised you both a nice lunch,' Sarah said, when she got close to them.

'Eh?' Nicky looked up. Elsa turned, unhooked the earplug and let it fall, leaned forward to switch the radio off. The faint but insistent music from the earpiece still sounded in the chill air, a frantic buzzing, like an insect's whirr of wings.

'Come on then,' Sarah touched both of them, her son on the shoulder, her daughter lightly, lightly on the top of her head. 'You two,' she said. 'When Tim gets back, let's get out of here, shall we? Let me find us find somewhere nice to go.'

# Acacia Gardens
## from a memoir

*Lynnda Wardle*

*ADOPTING A CHILD: 803. Both parents should want him very much. A couple should decide to adopt a child only if both of them love children and feel that they just can't get along without them. Dr Benjamin Spock's Baby and Childcare, 1955.*

They move to Acacia Gardens on Louis Botha Avenue. North Houghton, my father will say, not Hillbrow, it being important to stress from the start that they have always lived on the right side of respectable. Their flat is on the first floor of the squat building and has blank windows facing onto the main road. My mother sews thick curtains on her Singer, a wedding present, to block out the noise and dust from the traffic. Number 12 Acacia Gardens has no garden, not even a small quadrangle with a cheerful border that she has seen in other nearby buildings. There are no paths bright with pansies and African daisies, no scented jasmine climbing the walls. An Acacia tree stands alone in the front courtyard, ringed by a small metal railing.

. This is a new kind of life for them. Neither is used to living in such a confined space and without a garden. My father, having grown up on a farm in the Northern Cape is used to acres of blond maize with the Overberg mountains outlining his horizon. My mother has spent her life until now under the shadow of Table Mountain, the seasons defined by stiff Southeasters in the summer or damp winter Northwesters blowing in from the Atlantic. They have moved from Cape Town to Johannesburg because he has been offered a job. It is a *promotion*; my mother pulls her mouth to hide a smile when she tells this story, and I can tell she likes the sound of the word, its self-importance and promise. He was promoted, she says, from Window Dresser at Stuttafords to Marketing at the OK Bazaars. It was a big step up.

The step up means that they pack the little Austin with their wedding presents and suitcases and leave the Cape. My father carefully negotiates the overladen car through the drizzle towards the N1, the road that will take them nine hundred miles north. She rests her head against the car window leaving an unhappy smear, refusing to wipe her eyes. She cries as they wind through Paarl and up the DuToit Kloof Pass, the car struggling to pull on the incline even in first gear. She cries as the land folds down towards Worcester and into the Hex River Valley, eventually flattening into the Karroo. The scrubby desert flashes past hour after hour, volcanic outcrops against the blue Karroo sky like miniatures of Table Mountain to mock her. She cries through Laingsburg, Beaufort West, Hanover and Colesburg, until they reach Bloemfontein where they finally stop for the night. The hotel room is dark and she keeps the light off and her sunglasses on. She refuses to eat.

My father is the only diner in a large colonial style dining hall. He changes his clothes for dinner and eats surrounded by mahogany furniture and tables dressed with white linen. The waiter, a young Indian with fez and tassle, moves around the room, straightening cutlery and polishing glasses. A fan heater has been placed near my father's table for warmth but it has little effect against the cold of the Karroo night. My father finishes his roast beef, potatoes, jam roly poly and custard. He drinks a coffee and smokes. Eventually he returns to the room where she lies, eyes closed and awake, refusing to speak to him.

They couldn't be further away from their old life if they had boarded a ship and set sail for a foreign country. Even though they live in Johannesburg for the rest of their lives, she will never admit to any pleasure in this city and blames my father for tearing her away from her birthplace. She is inconsolable at its loss. Nothing can compare to the beauty of the Cape; the softness of its landscape, the smell of the sea, the wildness of a Southeaster blowing so hard that you have to hold onto a lamppost to stay upright or the sight of the cloud pouring over Table Mountain. Cape Town is the place of youth and promise, the place before things became difficult and complicated for her. If only she had been able to stay in the Cape she knows she would have been coaxed by its fertility; her womb would have flowered, producing children of her own, blue-eyed babies with golden hair like hers. This would have been her rightful family.

But instead, here she is in the autumn of 1960, resident with my father in a small flat in Joburg. The Highveld air is thin and dry, six thousand feet above sea level. The wind shakes leaves from the trees and the nights are turning bitter. He made me go, she says; and although the content changes slightly each time, the lament is the same. I never wanted to leave, she'll say. *He* made me go. She huddles in front of the two bar heater listening to the radio. There are crowds and guns and bodies lying in the streets of Sharpeville.

She is shocked and afraid. Coloureds would never behave this way, she tells my father. Coloured people are more civilized than these blacks. I don't feel safe here, Marius, she says when he comes in from work. These people are dangerous and before you know they'll be running down our streets too.

He disagrees. I don' think so bokkie, he says. The blacks in the townships here are just troublemakers. The government will put a stop to this kind of thing; we have nothing to worry about where we are. My father buys The Star every night and reads everything, improving his English while informing her about current affairs.

This whole shooting business is a gemors, he tells her. They've made a mess of things. They can't just shoot people in the back, it's not right.

At night, lying on her side of the bed, cold and anxious, she hears the scrape of branches against the roof as the trees shiver in the wind. It is the sound of her ovaries shrivelling like walnuts. Blood thick with clots streams out of her and one morning she faints fom the pain. After months of coaxing, she finally agrees to consult the specialist. Doctor Wells makes a small temple with his fingers and leans his elbows on the desk between him and my mother as he delivers his verdict. Surrounding him are photographs of his children and grandchildren displayed in brass and silver frames. Later that week, she is taken, I was *rushed,* she says, to hospital to have the whole sorry mess removed. She is only thirty-three when the hope of having her own babies is finally laid to rest in a silver dish by the surgeons who tell her as that in all their careers they have never seen such diseased ovaries. They tell her she will be much better without them.

My mother's recovery is slow. It will be six months before she pays any attention to what is happening around her and it will be a year before she is properly out and about. My father is desperate with worry. Contrary to what she first believed, my mother finds out they have left her with a slice of one ovary.

We thought we would give you another chance, Dr. Wells says at the first follow-up appointment. She returns home with this news, and both her and my father are bewildered at this sudden introduction of hope into their situation. Still, months go by and my mother drags herself around the flat, absent mindedly cupping her belly where the scar is healing nicely. Sometimes she watches the rush hour traffic from the small balcony, cars glinting in the morning sun and is surprised to find tears running down her cheeks. One evening she throws a heavy lamp straight at my father and he ducks as it smashes against the wall. She leaves him to pick up the pieces.

He consults the doctor on his own. Doctor Wells, making the little temple with his hands again, regards my father across the desk.

There is really nothing I can do Mr Neethling, he says. There is no reason for her not to be taking gentle walks and getting her life back on track.

She seems to be in constant pain, my father tells him.

This is unusual, says Doctor Wells. Bring her in next week and I will examine her again.

They return to Suite 226 Lister Buildings the following week, my mother pale and silent as ever, my father worried about taking more time off work. Doctor Wells directs her to the small cubicle where she strips down to her bra and panties and puts on the cotton gown. She worries about the gap at the back and holds the flaps together with one hand. The examination table is covered with a sheet of crackly paper that scratches the back of her thighs. She hears the doctor and my father murmuring in the room on the other side of the curtain. Their words are a low rumble and she can't pick out the meaning. She waits.

Right, says Doctor Wells, sweeping the curtain aside and closing it behind him. His hands are cool. He palpates my mother's abdomen and she tries not to cry out. He feels and presses, making soft grunting noises that she is at a loss to interpret. He strokes her scar.

You've healed up well Mrs Neethling, he says, pushing his glasses onto his forehead. Where is the pain? My mother struggles to explain. It's in here, she says, waving her hand over her belly. It's in there. Somewhere.

Doctor Wells slides his glasses back onto his nose and presses his fingers into her belly again, this time a little more vigorously. My mother lets out a small cry and my father winces in his seat.

That's fine, Mrs. Neethling, he says straightening up, tucking his glasses into his top pocket. You can get dressed now. She wants to ask him, what is it? Why am I not getting any better? But he has swung the curtain aside and returned to his desk to write on his notepad. He tears a page off and hands it to my father.

Pop down to the chemist on the ground floor and get her these, he says. This should do the trick.

The pain stays firmly lodged in her abdomen and my mother does not visit Dr Wells again. When the tablets are finished, she stores the plastic bottle in her dressing table with the lipsticks, but never asks for a repeat prescription. She doesn't tell my father of the strange burning sensation she has in her side when she wakes in the morning. She never mentions the ache that starts around midday and lasts until she finally lies down after supper. Long after he has fallen asleep, she lies stiff with panic. In a recurring dream she is in a small rowing boat somewhere in the middle of a lake. The horizon is clear but she stares into the distance, looking for clouds. In this dream she never has an oar.

At night, when my father tries to kiss her, she pulls away. At some time in their past they must have kissed properly, with tongues entwined and she must recall that feeling, but she does not want this from him anymore. His hands feel rough and she doesn't like them on her body. He tries every now and then to touch her gently, on the nape of her neck or to snake his arm around her waist, brush his lips on her forehead, but it is difficult to persevere in the face of such indifference.

What they cannot talk about is the loss that has lodged itself in the center of their lives. She had hoped for a big family and he had said this was his dream too. She had imagined it like a studio picture. The two of them circled by a clutch of boys and girls, various heights and sizes, freckles, brown hair, blond hair, scrubbed and in their best clothes for the picture. Everyone is smiling. She tells me another story, much later, about how she never loved him at all, how she married him because he was persistent and she was heartbroken over the loss of someone else. She tells me he wanted children as much as she did. It is not his fault that this cannot happen but still, it is as though he has betrayed their dream. It is unfair to blame him, but she does it anyway. He should have been able to make this family happen.

How does the idea of adoption come about? Does he speak to her one evening after dinner, while she nurses a whisky and ginger ale? What does he say? Perhaps this is a conversation they will have many times; he will come at the topic directly and slant, arguing all the angles. After all, she still has the hopeful bud inside her and month after month she waits for the bleeding that always comes. A fortnight after the bleeding ends, she allows him onto her side of the bed to lift her nightdress above her hips and lie on top of her. These encounters are over quickly and then he is back on his side of the bed again. He can never be sure when this opportunity will arrive and it must seem arbitrary to him, this permission and refusal. There can be no sense of closeness in the act, it is for making a baby and that is that.

Month after month though, as predictable as the seasons, her leftover ovary sheds its egg.

In the weeks approaching Christmas of 1961 my father begins his adoption campaign. He argues that it takes time to adopt a baby. There are waiting lists and they will have to put their names down on one (or many) of these. We don't have to commit ourselves, he says. If they offer us a baby and we are not ready, we can just say no.

I don't want someone else's baby my mother says, holding her side, the ache spreading into her back and down her legs. I want us to have a baby of our own.

Ja, I know, says my father patiently. I know, but this *will* be a baby of our own. We'll apply and sign all the papers and then it will be ours. My mother sighs and picks up the newspaper.

My father joins the Hillbrow library and borrows all the books he can find on adoption, requesting those that are in the catalogue but not on the shelf. Over a period of weeks he gets to know the plump librarian and they make small talk, never about the weighty matter that he cradles in his arms, but how hot it is this year and the severity of the last thunderstorm. He likes her. She is solid and friendly. He looks forward to his visits to the library which are uncomplicated and pleasant and prepare him for the silences at home. When he gets back to the flat, he leaves the pile of books on the kitchen table for my mother to read. She doesn't open them, but every night after their meal, he has his coffee and cigarette and settles down at the kitchen table to begin reading. He makes notes in a small notepad that he keeps on his bedside table.

How many weeks and months does this go on for? But at some point, my mother must show some interest. Perhaps he reads a passage to her one night that catches her attention.

Listen to this bokkie, he says, listen here. My father has come to rely on the kindly wisdom of Dr Spock in his campaign to win my mother over. He rubs his thumb along the inside of the spine and reads: *A couple should not wait until they are too old to adopt a child. They are liable to become too set in their ways. They've dreamed so long of a little girl with golden curls filling the house with song.*

And somehow this difficult thing, this taking on someone else's problem begins to appear for the first time as a solution to their own. She leans in closer and listens, trying to imagine carrying a small bundle from the hospital, perfect and readymade, warm and smelling of someone else's milk. It would be hers though. It would be theirs. That's what the books say, and slowly she inches towards an image of that baby in the hollow of their marriage.

Maybe, she says. Maybe we can look into it.

# Live at the Hidden Door Festival, Edinburgh, 2014

*Rob A Mackenzie*

Ross and I tracked down
the Vaults and chatted to
Andy and Brian in a circle
of writers, musos and artists.
Everyone was talking about
Janie, no one was certain
where she was hiding;
we knew she'd get there
but wanted badly to pretend
otherwise for a minute,
allowing our lives a certain
unpredictability. Janette was
by the entrance texting Colin,
I texted Janette and Janette,
a lioness, gave me a hug
as if I were an actual person.
Janie arrived on time, which
made us all feel not quite
wild enough, as Janette
suggested was my problem
later on, but Janie recited
her poem, a band initiated
the latest folk-rock revival
and Colin blagged entry for
half price. Janette and I
escaped to the bar, Colin
rolled joints on the table
and sipped his soda water.
Andy and his trio were live
on stage. People like me
leaned against the walls
and got covered in dust.

It was music only shadows
could dance to but no
shadows breached the dark.
I swayed, the dusty walls
stood firm. I downed a can
of Red Bull exactly like
MacAdam in Andy's poem.
Ross seemed quite drunk but
a good drunk; just as well
for an amateur boxing champ
and Brian's double-bass player
was hitting her instrument like
a drum, brushes and hammers
of all kinds, bubbling up some
experimental jazz improv
that Brian cooked poetry over,
but we couldn't stay for long.
Time to read my love poem
for two voices, a response to
*Different Trains* by Steve Reich
before the Viridian Quartet's
live performance. I bought
Janette a Jack Daniels, a lager
for me, and we read the love
poem which was also an end
of love poem. I asked the crowd
to decide which and Janette
provocatively asked, 'Are you
sure?' in the poem's final line.
I was not sure. The music was
great, those Viridians could
really play over twenty-seven
minutes: trains from New York
to Los Angeles, from Berlin
to Dachau, and after the war
the German soldiers' applause
for a woman's beautiful voice
echoing down a platform –
the woman invariably Jewish...

A short break for more drinks
and then a DJ set, dancing
before the rappers took over,
but by the time the rappers
rhymed *sky* with *die*
and offered the lines
    *could be worse*
    *could be in a hearse*
it seemed like the best
of all possible outcomes
for Colin, Janette and I
to prop up the bar once more,
to get drunk and stoned
and then find another bar
and another until words
eventually failed us as words
always do when faced with
an indescribable anti-climax
again and yet we felt a wild
kind of love, love for real,
even if love as a word often
fails us (let alone love for actual
people), but we felt somehow,
around 2.15am in the *Banshee,*
we had to be the greatest
people we had ever met.

# The Poetry Reaper

*Graham Fulton*

sitting in The Scotia
after John McGarrigle who-
was-killed-in-The Clutha's funeral,
wolfing
triangular tuna sandwiches
and listening to someone singing
*We Shall Overcome*
into a feedback microphone, I ask
Bobby Christie
if he remembers walking home
twenty-five years ago
from Tom Leonard's Writers' Group
in Paisley in the dark
with
towering orange streetlamps
and turning left into Penilee Road
where a cop in a panda
wound down his window and asked us
what we had in our bags
to which we shouted *POETRY!*
in unison,
lifted
thick majestic photocopies
and POEMS OF THIRTY YEARS
by Edwin Morgan into the air
as he looked on in horror
and told us to be on our way
and not to do it again

and Bobby
disappeared over the hill
as I turned right into Atholl Crescent
to go to a house where I no longer live
to talk to people who

are no longer there,
and Jim Ferguson
is wearing a burning red tie
and brandishing a virtual cigarette, and
*We Shall Overcome* was sung
by Joan Baez in 1963, it's really
hard to believe, it feels
as if yesterday
has still to happen, tomorrow
is already gone

# Secrets and Lies

## Pelmanism
*Dilys Rose*

Luath Press, RRP £12.99, 224pp

The secrets and lies of family life have long been inspirational for writers; from Sophocles to The Simpsons, and part of the success of these tales is due to recognition. Everyone has aspects of their familial relationships which are never openly questioned or discussed, or if they are it is usually too late. Dilys Rose's novel 'Pelmanism' is about the Price family as seen through the eyes of daughter Gala, but particularly it concerns her elderly father, Miles. As the novel begins, she is preparing herself to face him, possibly for the last time.

The title comes from a card game that Gala played with her gran, each of them trying their damnedest to lose to each other, but it is also the name of a memory-training system which was popular in the early part of the twentieth century, and it is memory that the novel is chiefly concerned with and which gives the book its structure. Gala remembers incidents with her father from her past, and the chapters move from memory to memory in a non-linear fashion, fragmented and incomplete.

At first I worried that the central characters were too one-dimensional; the overbearing father, the put upon wife/mum, the nourishing and supportive gran, and the daughter whose feelings for her father move from admiration, through disappointment, to outright contempt; but once you start to work through the multiple layers of Gala's memories it becomes clear that these are the roles which all are assigned by this family unit and it is often easier to play your part rather than try and change the whole. Rose is not looking at who they are, but why.

The driving force of the family dynamic is Miles Price, and how his family have to adapt to accommodate his hopes and aspirations, for little, or no, thanks or reward. He is an all too realistic and recognisable creation; a man who has come to blame his family for his life not turning out how he envisaged it. His two major obsessions are Marlene Dietrich and himself, and Marlene comes a distant second. He is the patriarch, and wants everyone to know that, but his rule is one which is not to be questioned or contradicted, and Gala is faced with the choice to accept this, or move away.

As the memories are revealed Miles is seen as a man who will go to almost any lengths to allow his delusions to continue. His one-man show of his painting, 'at the McLellan Galleries', sees his behaviour reach new heights of insensitivity as shown by his 'portrait' of his daughter, and how he deals with the passing of Gala's gran. You may think that this is a man who should be written off, but all of this is tempered by the knowledge that he is now old and ill, and also by the thought that memory can play tricks, which means that Gala's testimony is perhaps not the most reliable.

I may be the perfect reader for 'Pelmanism' as I am at the age where a lot of what unfolds is only too recognisable to me, both in the character of Gala, and the rest of the Price family, and I wonder if other readers will share this empathy as easily. But if they don't yet, they will as the book is also about growing up and growing old. Family ties are ties that bind, but often they bind too tightly and are impossible to escape. Dilys Rose reminds us that, when it comes to family, you can check out any time you like, but you can never leave.

– *Kes*

# Yearning for Youth

## I Put a Spell on You
*John Burnside*

Jonathan Cape, RRP £16.99, 288pp

If books were rivers, *I Put a Spell on You* would be the Great Ouse – meandering, slow and full of interesting little fish. John Burnside's memoir is deliciously written, with some truly beautiful passages. Interspersed are short musings/thoughtworms/digressions on various subjects. The first is on glamour – not the glamour of celebrities ('manufactured bedazzlement') but that of its old connection with magic and wonder. That glamour, Burnside suggests, is where love resides. These asides, given with the air of a man holding forth to his acolytes, are excellently wrought.

The memoir itself describes Burnside's many loves, flings, near misses and missed opportunities, each chapter of which is tied to a song with a particular resonance to the drama that unfolds, and which creates a form of mix tape that traces the emotional high-points of his youth. You don't have to be an aficionado of the sounds of the 60s to read the book, but having a device on hand

to play the songs as you read is well worth it. What it achieves best is that through this memoir you are shown a fresh view into the workings of this great poet; the fascinating digressions and mercurial narrative show the superb grasp of language on offer.

However, there is a rather ugly undercurrent to this memoir, which is, at a base level, a list of his conquests (or the ones who got away). Phrases such as, 'It's not often that I remember the faces of men or boys' do not help ameliorate this feeling. Also, at no point does Burnside bring his wife or children into the narrative; it is almost entirely a navel-gazing exercise, and though he has no reason to do so (it is his memoir, after all) there is a feeling that you have just been party to a particularly passive-aggressive attack on their relationship. Maybe the darker edges of his personality are so bared to show us all the clearer that 'the tedium of grown manhood' is society's fault, not his. I have not read either of his two previous memoirs, so cannot say if this is a continuing theme, but for me there was something all too predatory in his yearning for the sexual abandon of his youth.

Despite these failings, when Burnside's language catches, it burns bright, beautiful and supremely lyrical, and even when I was cross with him for his attitude and behaviour, I was still drawn deeper into the glamourie ('a charmed condition where everything, even the most commonplace of objects or events, is invested with magical possibilities') of his language, and those who choose to read this book will not be disappointed.

– *The Very Hungry Caterpillar*

# Changing Time

## Ghost Moon
*Ron Butlin*

Salt Publishing, RRP £8.99, 241pp

It has become something of a cliché for the reviewer to shake their head in bewilderment at the continued status of Ron Butlin as 'Scotland's Best Kept Literary Secret'. Each new publication adds evidence for Butlin's elevation to the pantheon of recognised Scottish greats and each subsequent book brings further disbelief that this hasn't happened yet. *Ghost Moon* is no different.

Maggie Davies is ninety and clasped by dementia. Her son, Tom – unrecognised by Maggie – visits her care home while her failing memory overlaps past and present. Neither are pretty. Pregnant, thrown out of her home for bringing shame on the family, spurned by all but her sister-in-law, Maggie is a smart and resourceful woman determined to resist the consequences of the label 'unmarried mother' and build a future for her and her son. As one character says in typical Butlin understatement: 'It isn't easy.'

Both narratives – a woman forced to fight for her own son and its mirror, the son fighting to be recognised by his mother – are deeply moving without ever becoming cloying or overdone. Butlin's wit and eye for the everyday intruding allows him to balance conflicting emotions. Tom, moved to nausea by both the smells of the care home and the pre-death grief he is experiencing can't help but notice the gorgeous Polish nurse. At the height of the most dramatic scene in the nov-el, Maggie shows a macabre sense of humour.

As is often the case with double narratives, one is more heavily weighted than the other. In this case, it's Maggie's past. We get brief snatches of Tom's life but it's primarily for context. These chapters, though slight, are nonetheless powerful. The second person, the 'you' so often deployed by horror and crime writers to bring immediacy to fear here serves to ratchet up the sickening sadness of his mother screaming 'I don't know you, get out.'

The two strands are carefully separated until the final chapter when, as Maggie approaches her own end, Tom is permitted access to the memories he previously assumed were rambling symptoms of her illness. The structural breakdown is deftly handled, the joins seamless.

We are in similar territory to Will Self's *Umbrella* but what Self does with Modernist firecrackers, Butlin achieves with understated empathy and the poet's sureness of phrase. Deep thematic imagery – illusions, time, correspondence – which would be neon-signposted by Self, are more subtly deployed. Butlin, who has no need for Self's smothering approach, allows the imagery to breathe.

Unlike *Umbrella*, *Ghost Moon* rejects nostalgia. Where the former ends with ghosts and empty rooms, Butlin ends at a beginning, an almost haiku moment of positive intensity. In the present Tom can't reach her but in the past they're always together. Their relationship is outside time. When Maggie left her parents' home, alone but for her unborn son, she stole the pendulum from the grandfather clock and launched it into the sea. From that day on, she keeps her own time.

– *Totoro*

# Visual feast

## Glovebox And Other Poems
*Colin Herd*

The Knives Forks And Spoons Press, RRP £8.00, 127pp

Art and design are major themes in this collection. Five of the more memorable poems are deceptively simple sequential instructions on how to draw an apple, bunch of grapes, milk carton, skull and toothbrush. These poems are triumphantly visual, leaving a lasting after-image on the retina – the dimple and stem of an apple, the fat heart shape. The images linger and project themselves onto the real objects. Poems in this style would work exceptionally well as a pamphlet accompanied by artworks. Here is a stanza from 'Apple':

> now i want you to kind of imitate
> that little dimple there but put it
> on top and then move all the way
> down kind of like a heart as if you
> were drawing a really fat heart

There are six poems on design: veil, rug, shoe, set, sweater and soap. These vary in format but most also have a strong visual element with delicious colours. Some require *in-group* knowledge or the willingness to Google. 'Veil Design', the first poem in the collection, only comes alive with the acquisition of a little knowledge about the work of Gareth Pugh and Issey Miyake. Other designers mentioned are Vincent Fecteau, Jim Jarmusch, Isaach de Bankolé, Kaj Franck, Peter Sloterdijk and Louise Bourgeois – all new to this reader.

There is a touching poem about the gay icon, Andrew Hayden Smith, about his last show on CBBC. It successfully conveys the precious nature of the nine-second, poor-quality recordings made from a television screen. Despite black lines and fuzzy images, the outpouring of affection for this openly gay presenter is compulsive viewing on Youtube. The poem ends with this extract:

> then he's in profile and a close up
> on his face. 6,753 times that clip's
> been watched and only ten by me.

Some of the other poems, including the title poem, 'Glovebox', probably fall into the category of Language Poetry. This movement began in the USA and its supporters include Ron Silliman, Lyn Hejinian, Bob Perelman and Rae Armantrout. This post-modern style is remarkably diverse and includes extreme forms of word play, fragmentation, decomposition of words and the absence of all connectives.

Herd frequently uses parataxis, leaving readers to construct their own connections between discordant fragments. It is difficult to tell whether these images have been carefully selected to convey a particular message or whether they are a random scattering of gems from the poet's notebook. Perhaps they are a mixture of both. Chance operations are embraced by many in 'avant-garde' poetry. Here is an extract from the titular poem, 'Glovebox'.

> parting issues
> speed bumps

slaw

hibsvhearse1996
doompuppy$
UsighonmeiSIGHonyou

risk otto
bury annie

A few days ago, I asked Don Paterson for his view on Language Poetry. His answer was characteristically succinct. He said, "It's rubbish". Herd himself is less succinct but just as dismissive in his opinion of traditional poetry. In an online interview with SJ Fowler, he complains about the fact that many poets "go on writing and supporting the writing of closed up pruney formal poems." I don't agree with Herd but I still enjoy the visual image evoked by 'pruney'.

The three most important aspects of poetry are semantic meaning, musicality and visual image. Herd is a very talented writer who provides wonderful visual images. He perhaps limits his readership by choosing to discard semantic meaning and embrace discordance to this extent. Still, I'd buy the book for the visual feast, the new way of seeing the shape of that apple.

– *Kanga the Kangaroo*

# Wonderful Stones

## Locust and Marlin
*JL Williams*

Shearsman Books, RRP £8.95, 80pp

If *Locust and Marlin* were a house, estate agents would describe it as 'full of character'.

Some of its rooms are cluttered with possessions and photographs, each with their own story to tell, while some are clean and full of light. The corridors that link these rooms are ones we all walk down, deciding how and where to live, and who to share our lives with. Edinburgh based poet, JL Williams, asks us to consider these questions in a beautifully structured second collection which, before we even get to the poems meets us with its gorgeous matt cover, a lino-cut I think, by the printmaker Anupa Gardner, which is soft to the touch and introduces us to the sensuous world Williams creates.

There is a sense of theatricality to the collection and poems featuring a heron bookend the collection like stage curtains. "Imagine a great silence / whose wings touch no branches. // Imagine a space demarcated / by lack of sound." ['Heron']

The backdrop has a mythic quality to it with a hint of bluegrass. There are underdogs and survivors who, like the fishermen in the book's titular poem, "were diagnosed one by one with disease / or crippling forgetfulness or pains / brought on by the drag of time's bright lure." And exist in heady, dreamlike imagery in 'Sargasso Sea': "Whose angels are women confined to river water, / Their hair green wool / Spooling in gin-clear streams."

In her epigraph, Williams quotes Gaston Bachelard from his seminal *The Poetics of Space*, a book on every art student's reading list, that I was very happy to be reminded of and revisit through poems considering shells and spirals. "One dreamer thought a shell was made / by a creature turning somersaults, each turn / a room for the home." ['Creation'] And securing the collection to the ground and in the body are stones, wonderful stones. "But don't you gold? / Do you quartz, crystal?" ['Stones of the West']

Williams is an enchanting reader of her work and a frequent collaborator and, having recently seen her spontaneously perform 'Stone Song' from this collection with a guitarist playing at the same event, I would highly recommend seeking her out and hearing her voice.

Reading *Locust and Marlin* put me in mind of the childhood game, blind man's bluff, having a scarf tied over my eyes and being spun by the shoulders. Images lap and weave together like the cover image and poems like 'Locust King' and 'Waltzer' feel vertiginous as they pull us up and away from earth, inviting us to look down at both the beauty and brutality of life, but all the time we are in safe hands and are shown moments of serenity, direction and, above all, love. "I left the world to find the world that we had lost / and lost the world again, as one must, perhaps." [The Veil]

– *Fiver*

# Friends Like These

## Head for the Edge, Keep Walking
*Kate Tough*

Cargo Publishing, RRP £8.99, 272pp

*Head for the Edge, Keep Walking*, the debut novel by Kate Tough, follows a year in the life of Jill Beech; a woman in her mid thirties forced to leave the familiar for the unknown; the day-to-day for the irregular; the safe for the adventurous.

Pushed into loneliness, Jill Beech is forced to re-evaluate her whole life after the break up of a long term relationship. Kate Tough provides us with a window into Jill Beech's dating experiences, friendships, health status, career choices and her innermost thoughts.

Jill Beech's life is seen through her eyes alone, jumping from scene to scene, connecting the funny, harrowing and nerve-wracking situations she finds herself in. Jill is a reflective character; the conclusions drawn from her reminiscing can be a little frustrating at times, however this is an enjoyable frustration because Tough has created a character worth caring about. I found myself talking to her in my own inner monologue.

The expressive and unexpectedly accurate metaphors Tough imagines make Jill's character so realistic you feel the urge to text her to meet for a mid-week glass of wine. It is a little like a fly on the wall documentary following one woman as her life changes through the course of a year, with the added bonus of her innermost thoughts: "Hilary handles her coat buttons like they're children who're taking too long over something."

Jill observes her friends closely in a caring yet critical way throughout her story, allowing you to 'know' her friends even if it is only through Jill's eyes. Early on in the novel Jill finds herself in her own company, filling the time by watching those around her: "I look around at people I don't know and make assumptions about them."

The most interesting thoughts she has are those that she would never say out loud, observations that in this reader/character relationship are interesting and strangely comforting. It is possible to know Jill in a way that we may not even know our closest friends.

I would like Jill Beech to be my friend. I lingered over some chapters because I wanted to spend longer with her. I read some chapters quickly because like a friend sharing gossip, I couldn't wait to discover what happened next. When Jill's story came to an end, I missed her; I wanted to know what she was doing... what she was thinking. This is not a typical break up book. Jill's unpredictable, frustrating, and funny life made me laugh, and cry, and remember. Just like a good friend.

– *Mrs Tabitha Twitchit*

# Puzzle of Grief

## Any Other Mouth
*Anneliese Mackintosh*

Freight, RRP £8.99, 260pp

Adventurous, vulnerable, and at times self-destructive heroines take central stage in Anneliese Mackintosh's debut collection *Any Other Mouth*. Upon reading three stories in a row, the characters' voices, vocabulary and worldviews seem exceptionally similar to one another. The plots, too, are made up of different moments in what seems to be a single life. Add to this the epigraph of the book "1) 68% happened. 2) 32% did not happen. 3) I will never tell," and the reader can't help but be seduced to play a game of hide and seek.

This game influences the act of reading: stories function as small pieces in a larger puzzle. A full-fledged portrait is being constructed, or so the reader thinks until 'A Rough Guide to Grief'. This painfully honest manual, that mocks new age survival books of its own kind, is one of the few stories that is not (strictly) in the first person and is the key that unlocks *Any Other Mouth*. All the stories in the collection lead to it, or grow from it, and can in fact be elucidated by it. Hence, despite the tempting biographic invitation, it is better to regard Mackintosh's collection as a map of sorrow: a young, outrageous, erotic, boisterous sorrow that matches its heroine.

Mackintosh is at her best when she dissects grief in its many shapes and forms; grief while deciphering other mouths, the grief of left over porn and burning cigarettes, the grief that hits you after death, welcome grief in the form of a shadow lover... The skewed decisions of Mackintosh's characters, that rise from or lead to grief, are not explained or excused, but rather presented lovingly and unapologetically. 'For Anyone who Wants to be Friends With Me' reminisces about rape, and is so painfully lucid, at times it proves difficult to read. 'If You Drank Coffee' imagines an uncaring lover as the ideal partner. The loneliness in both stories is disarming to say the least.

The flip side of the coin is that the grief Mackintosh analyses is of a certain kind. Unless the reader is happy focusing on different aspects of the same young, outrageous, erotic, boisterous grief in each story, the collection offers little variety. Tone and voice do not diversify. Characters echo each other. The locations do differ, but function only as background. This makes for a bleak narrative arc. One exception is 'You Are Beautiful'. Whilst it utilizes Mackintosh's trademark melancholy and mockery for new age rituals, the story seeks closure, perhaps even happiness, and ends on a self-accepting note. Peaceful or downcast, another strength of Mackintosh's is how she ends a story: her final words are consistently sharp and evocative. They linger.

In 'When I Die, This is How I Want It To Be', Mackintosh writes she wants her "regrets to be exhibited as *objects d'art.*" *Any Other Mouth* realises this wish. Mackintosh's work will appeal to those who like confessions of the intimate kind.

– *Departed Cat*

# Bitter Fallout

## The Dead Beat
*Doug Johnstone*

Faber & Faber, RRP £12.99, 272pp

Johnstone's latest thriller opens with 19 year old Martha Fluke on her way to her first day of work experience. Her route takes her through an Edinburgh cemetery, and a stop-off at her father's recently erected tombstone.

Death surrounds young Martha; not only the shadow of her estranged father's suicide, but her new role at *The Standard* newspaper turns out to be filling in on the obituary desk. The placement was set up by her late father, a journalist on *The Standard*, and so the people she is working beside in the now sparsely populated offices are his long-term colleagues. Like all print enterprises, *The Standard* and its sister paper are haemorrhaging staff, so what might have stretched the imagination in a previous decade – that a teenager with no experience is suddenly writing copy on a national newspaper – seems newly apt.

Martha takes a call from a weeping man who dictates an obituary to her – a shot rings out. The obituary is his own, and the man turns out to be the journalist she is filling in for. As Martha rushes to the man's house to try and save him, the book moves into its pacy stride: suspicious suicides, a legacy of guilt and grief, and Martha's own struggles with her own mental health issues.

Flashbacks take us back to the early 90s, when Martha's parents' fateful court-ship is enacted against a series of real-life gigs around Edinburgh and Glasgow. Johnstone's passion for documenting the details of long ago gigs in sweaty basements results in a certain tension between reportage and the necessary twists and turns of a thriller plot where everything must converge. As the deeds of the past inevitably play out in the present, the story closes in on the question of what happened on North Bridge one night in 1992 that caused such bitter fallout. The reveal of this incident is satisfyingly shocking and well handled.

As a sympathetic protagonist, Martha has perhaps too much of the stompy teenager about her – yo-yoing between cycles of ECT for her depression and impressive levels of alcohol consumption and mum-baiting in between. Issues of mental health and its possibly hereditary nature run throughout the book, sometimes freshly dealt with, as in the positive portrayal of electro convulsive therapy, or more conventionally when it enters 'madman on the loose' territory.

Like its predecessor *Hit and Run*, *Dead Beat* benefits from a vividly rendered setting in contemporary Edinburgh and some lean and punchy prose.

– *Shere Khan*

# Eucalypt Leaves

## A Wild Adventure – fragments from the life of Thomas Watling, Dumfries Convict Artist
*Tom Pow*

Polygon, RRP £12.99, 112pp

A healthy scepticism should be brought to any encounter with a book of poems which is explicitly "about" a person, object or place – especially one as little known as the story of Thomas Watling. What motivation does the poet have for using this device? Has he exhausted the liminal spark that is the originator of much poetry, and now needs to mine the experience of others unknown? But in Tom Pow's latest book, the remarkable life of Thomas Watling is no verse MacGuffin.

Taking as its starting point 26 year old Watling's arrest for the forgery of twelve one-guinea (about £5 today) notes in Dumfries in 1788, it tells – in tight and simple couplets – the fascinating story of his subsequent conviction, plea bargain (banknote forgery then being a capital offence), and transportation to New South Wales in 1791 where his ingenious draughtsmanship gained him freedom from hard labour in return for conscription as an indentured colonial artist. He spent eight years in the infant colony, feeding the ravenous appetite of the home audience for exotic illustration of the "age of wonder", before being pardoned in 1797 and working his way home to Scotland via several years in Calcutta making and selling miniatures.

The book is divided into four chronological sections covering Watling's arrest and trial, transportation, Indian experiences and eventual return to Scotland. Each of these is prefaced by extracts from the letters that Watling sent to his Aunt Marion – his de facto adopted mother since being orphaned in infancy. Pow's verse achieves the perfect balance between 18th century form and 21st century idiom and thankfully eschews the dry historical style and flowery language that this book could have suffered from in the hands of a lesser writer. As befits the story of a man who made the first oil painting of an Australian landscape, the viewpoint is chimerical and shifts between contemporary and current interpretations of this "first gulag", this "nation founded on gun, whip and cock". In doing so, Pow uses a wide range of imagery and allusion, with references ranging from the current Middle

East crises to the poetry of DH Lawrence and the films of Bill Forsyth. While much of Watling's life is available to history from his drawing, painting and letters, the seven years between his departure from Australia and his reappearance in Dumfries in 1804 are known only from census records, making them the perfect foil for some excellent poetic licence.

Perhaps the most affecting poems are the final ones concerning the time of Watling's return to Scotland in penury. These include a fascinating examination of similarities in the last letters of Watling and of Robert Burns – they were contemporaries in Dumfries in the 1780s and, Burns being an Exciseman, possibly knew each other. Burns died a year before Watling's departure from Sydney; and in 'The Adventurer Returns', the image of the crumbled eucalypt leaves in Watling's pocket "...between thumb / And forefinger, a few odourless crumbs. / Only his memories, unlike a lick / of these once sharp leaves of eucalypts, stick" captures wonderfully the interhemispheric sense of heimweh that those who have spent an extended period of time Down Under will know only too well.

– *Moby-Dick*

# Dear Gutter

*My partner is a feckless musician who has failed to embrace fatherhood and lives like a teenager instead.*

*My partner is in a band with his brother. They had some success a decade ago but the money has long since dried up. During those years I had a good time, travelling the world, meeting A-listers, living in the moment. We were in demand, invited into the homes of the rich and other interesting people. Eventually we settled and had children. While I recognise I was complicit in those years of freedom, enjoying the ride, when the kids came along I knew it was time to knuckle down. Unfortunately this has never occurred to my partner. He lives much as he did ten years ago, with no sense of obligation to provide either structure or support for his children. He had a bohemian upbringing and I cannot help thinking that, in the face of what could only be described as neglect, his loyalties lie with his music and his damaged brother rather than his own young family. Is it time to cut my losses?*

## Gutter says:

For many of us, we can look back at a single moment in our lives when we accepted real responsibility for the first time. For some it is the loss of a parent, for others redundancy or some other misfortune, that drags them into adulthood kicking and screaming. So often it's becoming a parent. Standing there, holding our own flesh and blood for the first time, we realise that this tiny, vulnerable creature's survival, both physically and emotionally, is dependent on us and us alone. And the only way to keep this baby alive is to prioritise its needs ahead of our own. This can be exhilarating, liberating and utterly petrifying. Sometimes there's an instant empathetic connection, a flood of maternal and paternal instinct. Sometimes it takes months, if not years. Or it can be the fear of being branded a 'bad' parent alone that motivates us.

By the tone of your letter, it seems that, prior to the birth of your children, you were something of a passive partner in this relationship. Being spliced with a creative person, it's easy to sublimate your own needs in the service of 'the work'. The professional creative can feel that, to succeed, they must serve their own talent ahead of all else. Like football players, the clergy or conviction politicians, they put their own peripheral desires to one side and honour their higher calling. Other things in life are viewed as distractions, temptations which must be resisted. And a life partner is expected to sacrifice too. Did this attitude set the tone for your relationship in its early years?

When a couple become parents teamwork is essential. It's joyous but can be exhausting, dull and unpleasant. Regardless of employment status, when one partner engages with responsibility and the other doesn't it can be unbearable. Much worse than being a lone parent. Being the one who, through practical demands, has to be the nag, the clipper of wings, is soul-destroying. It creates its own dynamic, a downward spiral of negativity, where you are cast as the spoilsport and they the oppressed.

I am assuming that you have already had brutally honest conversations where you have shared how you feel and what you want. Have you also asked him what he wants? I suspect that his responses have been unsatisfactory. It is important to break out of the roles you have fallen into if you can.

One solution would be shock therapy – although I don't recommend it. Abandoning your partner and children, even for a short time, might force his instincts to kick in. However, over and above the undoubted damage to you and children from such an arbitrary act, you also say he had a chaotic childhood and it may be that he actually lacks the basic skills to be a parent.

The second way to break the pattern is to ask yourself a difficult question. What is more important, companionship or equality? My guess is that a key issue is not just your partner's inability to provide but also his emotional disconnect from your own needs and goals, which are no longer subservient to his. That he is also locked into something of an adult-child relationship with his brother, as survivors of their shared childhood, further complicates things.

A lack of recognition and acknowledgment can be a deal-breaker. If you leave, you'll be on your own anyway. Is the relationship worth enough to abrogate him of all responsibility, accept that you will be sole carer, in the hope that, unfettered, he will be drawn back into family life.

To be honest, I doubt it. If the answer is no then it's maybe time to fly solo.

*If you have a problem you'd like advice on send it to deargutter@gmail.com*

# Contributor Biographies

**Dorothy Alexander** lives in the Scottish Borders. She writes in English and Scots and uses found techniques in much of her work. Her poetry has become increasingly visual and the featured piece was part of an installation resulting from collaboration with visual artist Linda Kosciewicz-Fleming for The Written Image, an exhibition curated by Edinburgh Printmakers and the Scottish Poetry Library.

**Janette Ayachi** (b.1982-) is an Edinburgh-based poet who graduated from Stirling University with a combined BA Honours in English Literature and Film Studies. Then after receiving an MSc in Creative Writing from Edinburgh University, she went on to publish in over forty journals and anthologies. She edits the online arts/literature magazine *The Undertow Review,* and reads her poetry at events around Scotland. She lives with her two young daughters; likes whiskey and wild women, and is the author of *Pauses at Zebra Crossings* and *A Choir of Ghosts.*

**Fran Baillie** promised herself that she would write more when retired and joined the MLitt at Dundee University. Best move ever! As a result she has had work published in *Gutter, Glad Rag, New Voices Press, Octavius, Dundee Writes* and anthologies and is presently working on a collection of Scots poetry. She is one of Jo Bell's gallant 52.

**Christopher Barnes'** first collection *Lovebites* is published by Chanticleer. Each year he reads at Poetry Scotland's Callender Poetry Weekend. He also writes art criticism which has been published in *Peel* and *Combustus* magazines.

**Henry Bell** is a writer and editor. He works for an arts festival; runs a regular night of music and poetry called Fail Better; and recently had some of he writing performed at a Play, a Pie, and a Pint at the Oran Mor. Over the last two years he has been working on cultural exchange projects between Scotland and Palestine. He lives in Glasgow.

**Liam Murray Bell** is author of two novels: *The Busker,* released in May 2014, and *So It Is,* shortlisted for Scottish Book of the Year 2013. He is Lecturer in Creative Writing at the University of Stirling and holds a PhD from the University of Surrey and an MLitt from the University of Glasgow.

**Robert James Berry** lives and writes in Dunedin, New Zealand. His poetry has been published widely. His ninth collection *Toffee Apples* is due out later this year from Ginninderra Press, Adelaide, Australia

**Jane Bonnyman** has been writing poetry for a few years and is a Clydebuilt 7 mentee. She has been published in *New Writing Scotland, Poetry Scotland* and in the National Galleries of Scotland *'inspired? get writing!'* 2013 publication. She has learnt to adjust to living sometimes in Glasgow and sometimes in Edinburgh

**Nick Brooks** was born and still lives in Glasgow. He achieved a First Class Honours Degree in English from Glasgow University, where he also graduated from the MLitt in Creative Writing. He has been studying for a PhD at the University of the West of Scotland. *Indecent Acts*, his third novel, was published in April 2014 by Freight.

**Jim Carruth** has had six acclaimed chapbook collections of poetry published to date. He has won both the James McCash poetry competition and the Mclellan Poetry Prize and been awarded a Robert Louis Stevenson Fellowship. Recently he edited an anthology of poetry for the Commonwealth Games and had his words etched in stone as part of Andy Scott's Kelpies project

**A C Clarke's** latest collections are *A Natural Curiosity*, (New Voices Press), shortlisted for the 2012 Callum Macdonald Award, and *Fr Meslier's Confession* (Oversteps Books). She was one of seventeen poets commissioned to write a poem for the Mirrorball Commonwealth Poetry Anthology *The Laws of the Game* and is currently working on a fourth collection.

**Craig Coyle** works in the Clydesdale area as a community psychiatric charge nurse, specialising in addictions. He has published in *Verse, Stand, Obsessed with Pipework, The English Chicago Review,* and *Fire.*

**Seth Crook** taught philosophy at various universities before moving to the Hebrides. He does not like cod philosophy in poetry. But likes cod, poetry and philosophy. His poems have recently appeared in Scotland's *Northwords Now, Gutter, The Open Mouse, Southlight, Other Poetry, Far Off Places.* And south of the border in such places as *Magma, Envoi, The Rialto, Orbis, The Journal, The Interpreter's House* and various fine e-zines. The world is his lobster.

**Ever Dundas** is a literary fiction writer specialising in the weird and macabre. She graduated from Edinburgh Napier University with a Masters in Creative Writing with Distinction. She recently finished her first novel, *Goblin,* and is embarking on her second. Ever's interests include Queer Theory and the relationship between humans and animals. Delve into her strange world here: bloodonforgottenwalls.wordpress.com

**Sally Evans's** latest and seventh poetry book is *Poetic Adventures in Scotland,* published by diehard. She is the Editor of *Poetry Scotland* and runs the annual Callander Poetry Weekend in September. She has lived in Scotland for 35 years and has connections with Newcastle, County Durham and the English Lake District.

**Jim Ferguson** lives in Glasgow. Website at www.jimfergusonpoet.co.uk. Recent publications, *Punk Fiddle* - a novel: *Songs to Drown a Million Souls* - poetry: contributor to *A Bird is not a Stone* - a Palestinian *Anthology,* and *One O'Clock Gun.* -- Still dancing. Available for readings.

**Graham Fulton** is the author of over fifteen pamphlet collections and six full-length poetry collections, the latest of which is *One*

*Day in the Life of Jimmy Denisovich* from Smokestack Books. A sequence of poems is to appear in *Pub Dogs of Glasgow* published by Freight Books later this year. Website www.grahamfulton-poetry.com

**Ewan Gault's** debut novel, *The Most Distant Way*, was published in 2013. His short stories have won a number of awards and been widely published. He lives in Oxford, where he works as an English teacher.

**Charlie Gracie** is from Baillieston, Glasgow and now lives near Stirling. His poetry and short stories have featured in a range of Scottish publications and his poetry collection, *Good Morning*, is published by diehard. He is currently working with painter Graham Tristram and composer Tom Dalzell on a collaborative project about the road from Glasgow to Callander.

**Kirsty Gunn** directs the Programme of Writing Practice and Study at the University of Dundee. Her new collection of short stories *Infidelities* is out with Faber later this year.

**Susan Haigh** is a student on the MLitt course at Dundee University. Although *Werewoods* is her first published poem, her short fiction has won a number of prizes and has appeared or is forthcoming in several anthologies and journals, including *Mslexia, Cadenza, Grey Sparrow Journal* (USA), *New Writing Dundee* and others. She is a regular contributor to *The Short Review*.

**Graham Hardie** is 42 and lives in Helensburgh. His poetry has been published in *Agenda, Shearsman, The Interpreter's House, Gutter, The New Writer, Markings, Nomad, Cutting Teeth, The David Jones Journal* and online at nth position, Ditch and morphrog. He currently works as a gardener.

**Diana Hendry's** most recent publication is *The Seed-Box Lantern: New & Selected Poems*. Her short stories have appeared in many magazines and anthologies and broadcast on Radio 4. She's published more than 40 books for children. In 2012 her young adult novel, *The Seeing*, was short-listed for a Costa Award and a Scottish Children's Book Award.

**Colin Herd** was born in Stirling in 1985 and now lives in Edinburgh. Publications include *too ok* (Blazevox, 2011) *Like* (Knives, Forks and Spoons 2011) and *Glovebox* (KFS, 2013). *Glovebox* was highly commended in the Forward Prizes. He has published over 60 reviews and articles on art and literature in publications including *Aesthetica Magazine, 3:AM Magazine, PN:Review* and *The Independent*.

**Tendai Huchu** is the author of *The Hairdresser of Harare*. His short fiction and nonfiction have appeared in *Warscapes, Ellery Queen Mystery Magazine, Wasafiri, The Africa Report, The Zimbabwean, The Manchester Review, Kwani?* and numerous other publications. His next novel will be *The Maestro, The Magistrate, & The Mathematician*.

**Andy Jackson's** collection *The Assassination Museum* was published by Red Squirrel Press in 2010. Editor of several anthologies; *Split Screen : poems inspired by TV & Film* (2012)

and its sequel *Double Bill* (due Autumn 2014), and a cycling poetry project *Tour de Vers* (2014). He also co-edited (with W N Herbert) an historical anthology of Dundee poetry titled *Whaleback City* (Edinburgh University Press, 2013). He is currently working on his second collection and also co-editing a book of modern clerihews.

**Vicki Jarrett** is a novelist and short story writer from Edinburgh. Her novel, *Nothing is Heavy*, was shortlisted for the Saltire Society First Book of the Year 2013. Her short fiction has been widely published and shortlisted for the Manchester Fiction Prize and Bridport Prize. Her story 'Ladies Day,' first published in *Gutter 09* appears in SALT's Best of British Short Stories 2014. www.vickijarrett.com.

**J. Johannesson Gaitán** grew up in Sweden and Colombia and currently lives in Edinburgh. She writes about translations at therookeryinthebookery.org, and for the magazine *Café Babel*. Her stories and poetry have appeared, or are forthcoming, in *The Stinging Fly*, *Structo* and *Brittle Star* among others. Both poems in this issue belong to a project about the notion of free time.

**Russell Jones** is an Edinburgh-based writer. He has published two collections of poetry: *The Last Refuge* and *Spaces of Their Own*, and is the editor of *Where Rockets Burn Through: Contemporary Science Fiction Poems from the UK*. A sequence of Russell's sonnets is due out with Prole Books in 2014 and a full length collection is being published with Freight Books in 2015.

**Rached Khalifa** teaches Literature and Philosophy at the University of Tunis al-Manar, Tunisia. He earned a PhD from Essex University in 2002. He has published widely on W. B. Yeats and other modern writers. Among his publications *The Filthy Modern Tide: Coloniality and Modernity in W. B. Yeats*; *The Poetics of Ideology in Yeats: Pastoral, Nationality and Modernity*; and *Emblems of Adversity: Essays on the Aesthetics of Politics in Yeats and Others*. He has also translated several works into English.

**Rob A Mackenzie** was born and brought up in Glasgow and lives in Leith. He has published two pamphlets (with HappenStance and Salt) and two full collections (both with Salt), the latest of which, *The Good News*, was published in April 2013. He is reviews editor of *Magma Poetry* Magazine.

**Martin MacInnes** has published fiction and reportage in several magazines including *Edinburgh Review* 134 and 138. He was an 'emerging writer' at the Edinburgh International Book Festival in 2013, and won a New Writers Award from the Scottish Book Trust in 2014. His long project is on natural history and identity.

**Ciara MacLaverty** was born in Belfast, educated on Islay and lives in Glasgow. She is a full-time mother with ideas of becoming a part-time writer. Her stories have appeared in *New Writing Scotland;* and her first pamphlet of poetry, *Seats for Landing*, was said to have 'an exactness, so acute, it is often funny as well as painful'. She blogs at ciaramaclaverty.blogspot.co.uk

**Lynsey May** lives, loves and writes in Edinburgh. Her fiction has found its way into a variety of anthologies and magazines and she was the recipient of a Scottish Book Trust New Writers Award in 2012/3.

**Jennifer McCartney** is the author of the novel *Afloat,* published by Penguin UK and a bestseller in Canada. Her writing has been broadcast on BBC Radio 4 and appeared in the *Globe and Mail, XOJane,* and *Joyland.* Originally from Hamilton, Ontario, she is a graduate of the Creative Writing MPhil program at the University of Glasgow, and is currently an editor and freelance writer in Brooklyn, New York.

**Beth McDonough** first trained in Silversmithing at Glasgow School of Art, spent many happy years teaching Art in various sectors including Special and F.E. Having completed an MLitt in Writing Study and Practice at Dundee University, specialising in poetry, she continues to work in mixed media, and much of her poetry centres around the themes of maternity and disability.

**John McGlade** is a freelance writer from Glasgow. He scripts satirical and comedy material for television, radio and theatre shows across the UK. He writes stand-up for leading comedians, and also poetry which he performs around Scotland.

**Ross McGregor** is a previous recipient of the Scottish Book Trust New Writer's Award. He has had poetry published in *Gutter, New Writing Scotland* and *Algebra.* He also writes fiction. Ross lives in Ayrshire, Scotland.

**Carol McKay's** stories have appeared in many literary magazines, including *Gutter* 1 and 9, *Mslexia, Chapman* and *Southlight.* PotHole Press publish her collection *Ordinary Domestic.* Carol is an Associate Lecturer in creative writing at The Open University, and she reviews fiction and life writing for *Booktrust* and *Northwords Now.* In 2010, she won the Robert Louis Stevenson Fellowship.
carolmckay.co.uk

**David McKelvie** is in his late 30s and lives in Greenock. He has a background in mathematics, mapping and moping around. Currently, he writes for an audience of children. (@deemikay)

**Andrew McLinden** lives and works in Glasgow. His fiction has been nominated recently for a Pushcart Prize and twice nominated for a Gertrude Stein Award. He continues to work as a lyricist and his songs have appeared in a variety of film and TV projects.

**Wendy Miller** is a Glasgow-based writer. She writes plays and poems as well as teaching creative writing in HMP Barlinnie. Wendy wrote and directed Even In Another Time and co-wrote and directed The Bridge, both performed as part of Glasgay! She is currently working on her latest play, Baby Steps. She also loves music, photography and red wine.

**Stuart A Paterson** was born 1966 & raised in Ayrshire in a Scots language household. Poetry widely anthologised in the UK & beyond. *Saving Graces* was published by Diehard in 1997. Recipient of an Eric Gregory Award (Society of Authors) in 1992 & a Robert Louis Stevenson Fellowship (Scottish Book Trust) in 2014. Lives & works in the Stewartry by the Solway Coast.

**Tom Pow's** *Threads from a Dying Village* is the last of a series of short works related to *In Another World – Among Europe's Dying Villages* (Polygon 2012). *A Wild Adventure - Thomas Watling, Dumfries Convict Artist* was published in July and *Concerning the Atlas of Scotland and other poems* will be published in August (both from Polygon).

**A P Pullan** is originally from Harrogate, North Yorkshire and is now living in Ayrshire. Poems have been printed in numerous magazines including *New Writing Scotland* and *Cabshair/ Causeway*.

**Maggie Rabatski** is originally from the isle of Harris but she has made her home in Glasgow for many years. She has published two poetry pamphlet collections, *Down From The Dance/An Dèidh An Dannsa* and *Holding,* both with New Voices Press. She is a previous mentee of the Clydebuilt poetry mentoring scheme and she writes in both Gaelic and English.

**Dilys Rose** has published ten books of fiction and poetry, and has received various awards for her work. Recent collaborations include the libretto for the opera *Kaspar Hauser: Child of Europe*, composed by Rory Boyle. She is programme director of the new online distance learning MSc in Creative Writing at the University of Edinburgh.

**Mike Russell** is deputy editor of the *West Highland Free Press* newspaper and a graduate of Glasgow University. His fiction has appeared previously in *Gutter* and also in *Northwords Now.* His first novel is due to be published by Polygon in spring/summer 2015.

**Mike Saunders** has been published in various journals including *Lighthouse, Poetry Review, Dactyl* and the *Istanbul Review*. He previously organised the archival interview series Conversations in Black and White, and co-curates the websites Indian Litter and Happy Friday. He lives in Edinburgh.

**Alison Scott** was born in the Western Isles where she spent her early childhood before moving to Easter Ross. She now lives in Aberdeen where in recent years she has begun to develop her writing, especially her poetry.

**Hamish Scott** was born in Edinburgh in 1960 and now lives in Tranent, He has been published in various magazines.

**Kathrine Sowerby** is a Glasgow based poet with a background in fine art. A graduate of Glasgow School of Art's MFA programme and Glasgow University's MLitt in Creative Writing, her poems have been widely published and awarded prizes including a New Writers Award from the Scottish Book Trust. Kathrine makes *fourfold,* a curated journal of short poetry. kathrinesowerby.com

**Dan Spencer** lives in Glasgow with his wife and small daughter.
danspencerwriter.wordpress.com

**Judith Taylor** comes from Perthshire and now lives and works in Aberdeen. She is the author of two pamphlet collections – Earthlight, (Koo Press, 2006), and Local Colour (Calder Wood Press, 2010) – and in 2013 she was a runner-up in both the Cardiff International Poetry Competition and the Herald McCash Poetry Competition.

**Sheila Templeton** writes in both Scots and English. A first prize winner in both the McCash Scots Language and the Robert McLellan poetry competitions, she was also Makar of the Federation of Writers Scotland 2009 to 2010. Her two latest collections are *Digging for Light* New Voices Press 2011 and *Tender is the North* Red Squirrel Press 2013

**Eleanor Thom's** debut novel, *The Tin-Kin* (Duckworth, 2009) is out now. It is a novel based on photos, artefacts and memories of Eleanor's mother's Travelling family. A chapter of *The Tin-Kin* won the 2006 New Writing Ventures Award for fiction and it was awarded The Saltire Society First Book of the Year Award in 2009.

**Lynnda Wardle** grew up in Johannesburg and has lived in Glasgow since 1999. In 2007 she received a Scottish Arts Council grant to work on a novella about Africa. She has had poems and stories published in various magazines, most recently in *thi wurd* and *Gutter*.

**George T. Watt** was born in Clydebank, raised in Edinburgh, but lives in Dundee. He started his working life on the Island of Islay in the Inner Hebrides and on farms in the north east of Scotland. Graduating with 1st Class honours in Literature in 2006, with the Open University he writes almost exclusively in Scots and is published in, *Lallans, The Ileach, New Writing Scotland* and *Gutter*. He has also published two pamphlets, *Abune the Toun* and *An Ulster Triptych*.

**Ross Wilson's** poetry and fiction has previously appeared in *New Writing Scotland, Edinburgh Review, Anon, Horizon Review,* and many other magazines and anthologies. His first pamphlet collection, *The Heavy Bag,* was published by Calder Wood Press in 2011. He also worked as a writer and actor on The Happy Lands, an acclaimed award winning feature film.